TRAN
A Sho

CW00662067

TRANSYLVANIA
A Short History
by István Lázár

Corvina

On the cover
Sándor Ligeti Wágner: King Matthias returning from hunting.
The Castle of Vajdahunyad is in the background. 1880's
Budapest, Hungarian National Gallery

Translated
by Thomas J. DeKornfeld

Published in 1997 by Corvina Books Ltd.
1051 Budapest V., Vörösmarty tér 1, Hungary
Corvina Books Ltd. acknowledges
the assistance
of the Hungarian Book Foundation
(Magyar Könyv Alapítvány)
© István Lázár
Translation © Thomas J. DeKornfeld
ISBN 963 13 4333 2

Printed on 80gsm Biancoprint paper manufactured in the
Dunaújváros paper-mill

Design by Malum Stúdió
Printed in Hungary, 1997

Table of Contents

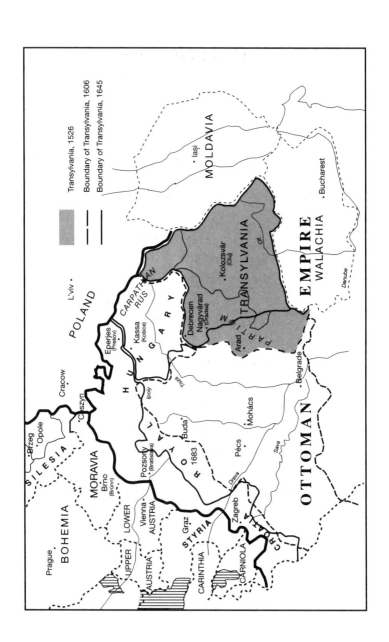

Prologue

*T*ransylvania, with its deep valleys surrounded by a coronet of peaks, its wide basins and highlands, pine forests and the Alpine meadows at the feet of imposing glaciers; with its salt mines already worked in prehistory, with its gold gathered since Neolithic times from veins in its rocks and from the waters of its streams; with its refreshing, acidic, wine-like, naturally carbonated springs, Transylvania, a small area in the lap of the Eastern and Southern Carpathians, is a country on the easternmost edge of Central Europe. Even though it was approached early by Eastern Orthodoxy emanating from Byzantium, its Christianity is basically Western. Initially the Roman ritual was predominant but later it became the bastion of European Protestantism.

Transylvania, this land protected by its mountains but accessible by its passes and open valleys, was overrun, ravished, conquered and reconquered. It was the historic apple of Eris between its original inhabitants and the conquering Hungarians, between the Hungarians and the Turks, between the Turks and the Austrian Habsburgs, between the Austrian Habsburgs and the Hungarians and between the Hungarians and the Romanians. Transylvania is the land of a remarkable people whose language is Hungarian, but who are distinctly Székely, and who consider themselves descendants of the Huns. According to the legends of their origin, they are the long awaited children of Prince Csaba, one of Attila's sons, who came along the Highway of the Armies, the Milky Way of the Heavens. This myth of their national origin is well-appreciated in the other parts of Hungary as well, but it is nowhere as strong as here. The dilemma of their true origin can not be discussed here, but it should be mentioned that their centuries-long role as guardians of the borders can be documented not only in Transylvania. There were Székelys along the no-man's lands separating nations and countries in southern and western Transdanubia, near the foothills of the Alps, in Pannonia, next to the southern Slav-German (Austrian-German) ethnic groups, as well as in the north, along the contemporary Slovakian-Ruthenian (Carpatho-Ukranian) border. The origin, history and fate of the Csángó-Hungarians, who were pushed beyond the Carpathians and who were there slowly broken up, is a historical question, allied to that of the Székelys. Their remnants, mired in Moldavia, still use a medieval Hungarian, just as though some hidden, detached fragment of a Serb or German population had kept old Slavic or Teutonic alive in their daily speech.

Transylvania is the native land of independent, towering individuals. This is whence Sándor Kőrösi Csoma started out toward the East, searching for the original home of the Hungarians and marooned in a mountain monastery in Tibet, uncovered the secrets of the Tibetan language, previously unknown in the West. It was in Transylvania that the son of Farkas Bolyai, János Bolyai, spent most of his life and "created a new world out of nothing" by independently delineating absolute geometry, anticipating most forcefully Einstein's theory of relativity. It was this land that Count Samu Teleki, the passionate hunter and explorer returned to from Africa, the only Hungarian traveler whose name is associated with the discovery of large tracts of "terra incognita". All were remarkable eccentrics, native geniuses of the forests and the crags.

Transylvania was an independent principality for barely 150 years and yet, in 1568, at the Diet in Torda, the assembled representatives enacted into law the principle of religious freedom, unprecedented in Europe at that time and for very many years thereafter. For the readers and movie-goers in Europe and around the world, Transylvania is the secret and mysterious refuge of Dracula, the monster hiding in the blood-stained ossuary of a casemated castle among the lightning-torn, ghost-ridden mountains. We consider Dracula as a specter born of a diseased imagination, and that is exactly what he is, although there are traces of a historic model for his existence. In one of the most beautiful Székely ballads, the masons were unable to keep the walls of Déva castle from crumbling until they drained the unresisting wife of mason Kelemen of all her blood, burned her lily-white body and mixed her ashes with the mortar. Then and only then would the stones hold and the walls rise. Béla Bartók drew many of his ideas from Transylvanian, Hungarian and Romanian folklore. His opera, "Bluebeard's Castle", with all of Bluebeard's former wives immured in their rooms, takes place among the mountains of Transylvania. One thing is certain: the soil of Transylvania has always produced more myths than wheat. Among the fateful storms of history and in the frequent famines, only a people having a rich and vivid imagination could survive. In the recent past, Transylvania again became the center of a fiction that must be classified as a myth. The Romanian ethnic group, late in developing into a nation and into a realm, based its national pride on its mid-Balkan roots and made the hypothesis of the continuous evolution of its Daco-Roman descent not only a part of, but the actual basis of its national and popular ideology.

The borders of Transylvania can be determined accurately by the geography of its mountains and rivers, both historically and administratively. Politically and ethnically, however, in the present Romania, these borders are more uncertain, more vague and in fact are forcibly obscured and eliminated. For a millennium the early Slavic and other nationalities were accommodated roughly in this sequence – Hungarian, Saxon, and Romanian people. Even though there were numerous conflicts among them, they coexisted so that again and again there was hope for tolerance and for a joint development so essential for mutual advantage. Yet, in this century and, particularly, during the second half of this century, there was a sharp increase in the Romanian endeavors toward the complete assimilation or annihilation of the Hungarian, Saxon and other extra-Transylvanian Romanian nationalities. This created a serious crisis affecting all of Europe. Transylvania was called a "Fairy Garden" and was considered an experiment in the history of East-Central Europe. In fact, more frequently, it was a small but threatening, inflamed and purulent wound on the body that was Europe.

Transylvania
is Far from Mesopotamia

*I*t is easy to draw Transylvania's natural geographic boundaries. The region lies in the mighty embrace of the crests of the eastern and southern Carpathians. It begins in the north at the sources of the river Tisza and extends in the south to that stretch of the Danube which once again flows in an easterly direction, and which by snuggling up to the southernmost tip of the Carpathians, separates the Carpathian and Balkan mountain systems. Its western boundaries are formed by the rivers flowing toward the center of the Carpathian basin. They emerge among their own detritus from the valleys of the central, isolated Transylvanian mountains, and both to the north and south of these mountains from the Carpathian ranges. Thus, it is enclosed on two sides by mountains, traversed only by nearly intractable passes, and on the third side by rivers and, formerly, extensive marshy areas. This conception of Transylvania as a geographic entity is currently widely accepted in Hungary. It is inaccurate and, more importantly, not historically correct. The term Transylvania may be used today to define three distinct territorial entities. There is a geographic Transylvania. It has an ideal shape and is a geographically homogeneous basin surrounded by well defined mountain ranges with an area of approximately 57,000 square kilometers. We can talk about a historic Transylvania with a variable area which in the 17th century, as an independent principality, extended far beyond the boundaries of the geographic Transylvania. The attached areas were referred to as Partium. This Partium shifted back and forth between the Kingdom of Hungary and the Principality of Transylvania. The third Transylvania is the area that was assigned to Romania by the peace treaties of the 1920s, and which today still forms a part of Romania. This area is larger by 46,000 square kilometers than the geographic Transylvania and encompasses a total of 103,000 square kilometers.

The geographic Transylvania has magnificent natural boundaries. In the east and south we find the continuous 1,500-2,000 meter high walls of the Carpathians, while in the west there is the massive block of the Bihar mountains. This bastion is traversed by three wide, easily passable gates, all three of them pointing toward the west, toward the Hungarian Great Plains. They are the gate of the Szamos valley, the Meszes gate leading to the Berettyó region, and the gate of the Maros valley. The Carpathians and the Bihar mountains are traversed only by a few narrow passes, across extensive, poorly populated areas. In the lap of the great mountains there is a central basin, the Mezőség, and a hilly area fragmented by rivers, the Küküllő region. There is also a whole range of small, peripheral, mountainous basins among the ranges of the Eastern and Southern Carpathians, and in their foothills. Outside of the historic Transylvania, there is a wide segment of the Hungarian Great Plains, given to Romania in the 1920s, now also referred to as Transylvania and extending from the plains to the watershed along the crest of the mountains. This region does not consist of adjacent, compatible parts and each part has a natural affinity toward a different area of the Great Plains.

At this point, however, we have advanced far beyond ourselves. As we turn to the beginnings of the historic development of Transylvania, let us return to the natural geographic considerations. Transylvania's valleys are in some places only 200-300 meters above sea level, while the surrounding and central peaks rise to heights of 1500 to 2500 meters. Its climate is determined by its low average temperature and by relatively copious precipitation. This favored a hunting and grazing economy, while it was less favorable to agriculture. The latter is also limited by the contours of the land and by the relative poverty of the soil.

According to the earliest archeological findings, in ancient times Transylvania was a well circumscribed area, occasionally bypassed by ethnic and economic movements, but in which external forces or settlements, produced a transient but specific internal cultural environment, and led to tangible progress. Yet everything that can be found in Transylvania today and that can be subsumed under the heading of prehistory, is not sufficiently specific or detailed to warrant inclusion in this brief summary. It may suffice to say that the Neolithic evolution, which showed marked Mediterranean influences, suffered repeated and marked stops and regressions. Even though the domestication of animals did take place, hunting and the consumption of game was still significant. This can be easily explained by the environment. (It may be mentioned here, that very many years later the last European bisons and aurochs in the Carpathian basin were killed in Transylvania, and that the Carpathian brown bear can still be found in the forests.)

The historic spotlight shone, albeit briefly, on this region after the discovery of the famous artifacts in Alsó-Tatárlaka, which showed pictographic writing and which were dated to 4000 B.C. It may be assumed logically that the local evolution in the Transylvanian area at that time led the inhabitants to a level of specialization and social stratification that required a system of permanent, written means of communication, and thus the introduction of writing. The Tatárlaka tablets are not unique. Their interpretation is supported by other pictograms dating to the same period, which had never been viewed in this light, and which suggest the evolution of a high civilization, extensive both in space and time and centered on the Vinca-Tordos Culture located in the Banate-Southern Transylvania region.

What is there in this period of the Transylvanian Neolithic age – already leaning toward the metal and early Bronze Age – which would permit that the Tatárlaka written tablets be interpreted as being indicative of an early, high civilization? We encroach here on an enormously complex problem. Is the Transylvanian Neolithic culture the result of an independent evolution, or is it inseparable from the Mediterranean Fertile Crescent evolution? In any case, it represents the existence of an astonishingly mature early Balkan metal culture.

In the wide-ranging and complicated archaeological debate dealing with as yet insoluble chronological dilemmas and arguing whether the evolution of the various early cultures was independent or interdependent, whether they developed in isolation or whether they learned and borrowed from each other, one thing appears to be certain. The advanced Balkan metal culture produced gold and electron (gold-silver) masterpieces, found in the Várna area since 1972, which in their sum total equal the esthetic and historic significance of the Tutankhamen treasure or of pre-Columbian gold. It could not have developed without either extensive exploitation of the Aegean or Transylvanian metal ores and the exportation of the precious metals from the mines to the heartland of the Balkans. We believe that Transylvania was the source of these ores. Yet, even if the ores came from the Aegean, the history of Transylvania shows that this area served as the source of discord for a variety of peoples, and that this was due primarily to the salt mines and to the mining of certain metals, namely gold, silver and, most importantly, copper, which can be dated back to the Neolithic era.

The great step forward documented by the Tatárlaka findings was, however, only temporary,

and the speculations linking Transylvania to Sumer
are without foundation, as is the idea that Transylvania
was the cradle of Sumerian civilization, and that the
native "pre-Hungarian" people were the sires of the
civilization in which the prehistory of man was
turned into the history of humanity. This "theory"
was developed and propagated as the completely
erroneous Hungarian answer and as a spiteful reaction to the equally fantastic Romanian hypothesis of
the Daco-Roman continuity. The further, sometimes
slow, sometimes more vigorous, but never complete
exchange of populations was the at times peaceful,
at times violent fusion of migrating peoples who
belong to a historic framework in which even the
name of the tribes is unknown. The neighboring and
sequential cultures can be separated only on the
basis of certain indicators of their ethnicity, found in
their burial grounds. It should be mentioned, however, that when the extensive Bodrog-Keresztúr culture, preferring the less wooded areas, was expanding toward Transylvania, even though the natural
environment was not favorable for it, the motivation
for this expansion is clearly shown by its use of copper, which was highest in the settlements closest to
Transylvania and least in the settlements farthest
from it.

Over the years, eastern pastoral tribes repeatedly
invaded the Late-Neolithic and the copper and
Bronze Age people of this region. The animal husbandry of these tribes was also a Neolithic achieve-
ment, but represented a less effective production of
food than that of the early agriculturists. The bel-

ligerence and mobility of these tribes temporarily overshadowed the advantages of an agricultural economy. There was also a time when these pastoral people completely overwhelmed the developers of the Transylvanian metal mines, and the latter withdrew from their settlements to caves in the mountains.

Who Were The Dacians and What Became of Them?

*D*uring its prehistory, Transylvania never had a homogenous population and was divided into smaller, temporarily isolated areas. It was about 2,500 years ago that the first society appeared which, based on its burial customs and other remains, seems to have inhabited the entire Transylvanian region, and for which we can find a name. The findings indicate that these people were related to the Scythians. Herodotos refers to them under the name of Agathursos. During their expansion, they even appeared on the eastern edge of the Great Plains. They also continued the Transylvanian tradition and had an advanced metal culture, which is no longer considered to belong to the Bronze Age. The Agathursos supplied the people surrounding them with iron weapons. They became fugitives during the fourth and third centuries, victims of the arrival and territorial conquests of the Celts.

Following the transient dominion of the Celts and in spite of the permanent residence of many of their people, the Dacian era of Transylvania and of a significant portion of the Carpathian basin had arrived. It is a particularly difficult era to discuss. Everything connected with them belongs to the highly sensitive area of the prehistory of the Romanian people and of modern Romania. From a Hungarian perspective, this fact makes this entire matter a delicate and highly controversial issue.

The prehistory and origin of these people, who came from Thrace, who slowly advanced from the Balkans northward and who had active and lasting contacts with the Greeks, remain obscure and much debated. This happens to be true for most European nations. The genesis of their Neo-Latin language is a peculiar and specific problem. They presumably infiltrated into Transylvania primarily from the Great Plains area of the Carpathian basin, although their "conquest" may have originated from several different areas simultaneously.

Dacian society itself was internally sharply divided into two groups. The elite group, the "cap wearers" or more accurately the "Fur Hat People" were the aristocracy which lived in mountain fortresses, well supplied with expensive imported Greek goods. Their subjects, the "Longhaired People", had their poorer and more defenseless dwellings in the open country. The outstanding personality among the Dacians was King Burebista, who ruled for as much as four decades during the first half of the first century B.C. The foundations for his strong administrative organization and stormy conquests may have been laid down by his father. This is similar to Hungarian history where (Saint) Stephen I only completed the initiatives of his father, the great Prince Géza, and yet Stephen is considered as the founding father of the country.

Under Burebista Dacian rule extended far beyond Transylvania. In the east it reached the Greek cities along the Black Sea. In the west, it extended to Transdanubia and to parts of the area of the present Slovakia. In the south, it encompassed Macedonia and the Adriatic. Thus, about half a century before the birth of Christ, the Roman Empire had to view the Dacian Empire as its greatest foe in the Balkans. Yet this empire, which very rapidly conquered a large number of tribal groups, was just as fragile as many other powerful organizations of antiquity.

The first major confrontation between Rome and the Dacians should have occurred during the rules of Caesar and Burebista. The situation was ripe for it. Both rulers, however, were eliminated by a political conspiracy and "regicide". The showdown between the two powers, Dacian and Roman, was critical for the control of the vital Middle and Lower Danubian space, and could thus be only delayed but not ignored. The causes and conduct of the conspiracy against Julius Caesar are well known from Roman historiography. Burebista's fate is much harder to elucidate. He most probably fell victim to his greatest accomplishment, the unification of the Dacian tribes, which inevitably led to the curbing of the jealously guarded prerogatives of the tribal leaders. (*Nota bene,* Burebista's administrative problems may have been similar in many respects to the problems encountered 1000 years later by the Hungarian Stephen.)

The rapid disintegration of the Dacian Empire following the murder of its charismatic leader, does not mean that we no longer have to be concerned with the Dacians. Rome, much beset by problems, slowly but consistently proceeded in strengthening its position in the northern Balkans and in East-Central Europe to ensure the flanks of its Eastern conquests, which now extended to Mesopotamia. Heading northward from Illyricum, it brought the Pannonian tribes under its rule, encompassing all of Pannonia, which corresponds to the entire present Hungarian Transdanubia. In a northeasterly direction it moved toward the Iron Gate in order to eventually control the entire lower reaches of the Danube. During this period it preferred to live in peace with the Dacians, rather than fighting them. In order to maintain this peace, it made major financial sacrifices and offered and provided technical assistance as well.

It is important to digress at this point and to mention the unusually significant changes which took place at this time of continuous national dislocations, in the lap of the Carpathian basin, in the Great Plains. This area was infiltrated from the north by Sarmatian tribes who settled this region permanently, ruling over and mingling with the local Celts, Dacians and other minor groups. This new Sarmata homeland inevitably became a buffer zone between the rulers of Pannonia in the west and of Transylvania in the east. This was true even on those occasions when the Sarmates themselves accepted and earned Roman pay as, for instance, when they built the "ditch and dike" Roman defense system which spanned the entire Great Plains and was known as the Devil's Ditch. At other times, however, either independently, or in league with the Transylvanian Dacians, they endangered the peace of Pannonia and repeatedly struck across the Danubian frontier. After the century-long fragmentation which followed the murder of Burebista, a new and eminent Dacian leader, Decebalus, who ruled from 80 to 106 A.D., again united the tribes of his nation. Thus – seen in the clear light of retrospection – it appears that the preparations of the Romans against the Dacians were delayed for too long. The Roman sacrifices, made for temporary peace, had been totally useless. It is a fact that shortly after his appearance in the 80s, Decebalus's armies inflicted several humiliating defeats on the Romans. The new Dacian ruler could blackmail the Romans and the revenues of such blackmail further strengthened him and his rule. It was only in 101-102 that the great Dacian campaign of Trajan reversed the Romans' fortunes of war. The Dacian power, recently so expansive, was stopped, withdrew and was forced on the defensive, at least temporarily. To insure the supplies for his legions and for the security of his logistic organizations, Trajan built the first permanent bridge across the Danube at the present Turnu-Severin. This facilitated the definitive victory of the new, 105-106 campaign.

Even though we don't share all the current Romanian enthusiasm for him, Decebalus was clearly an outstanding figure of this age. The fact that an enormous amount of gold, hidden during his time, was found, partly already in Roman times and also very much later, may perhaps lead to the not unwarranted conclusion that if Decebalus had not hoarded and hidden his gold, but had used it to increase his military strength and to buy allies, the Dacian campaigns of Trajan may have turned out quite differently.

On the other hand, the Dacian king could be described as a "Roman character". He knew well the fate of the loser. He knew that he would be taken to Rome by the victorious legionnaires like a captured animal, and there dragged along in the triumphal march in front of the hysterical multitudes. For reasons unknown, he could not escape the pursuing Roman mounted troops and on their arrival, he killed himself. It was only his head that they could take to Rome.

The Provincia Dacia was established in 107 A.D. This Roman occupation, protruding into the present Transylvania, or rather into its natural geographic unit from below, fell far short of filling up the entire eastern bay of the Carpathians. The northeastern part of Transylvania, the upper Tisza region was not included. And, although the Romans used the Carpathians in the east as a line of defense, it was not the crest that they used, but an interior line. The southern border of the province was provided largely by the lower Danube. This border was of less importance, since here the province abuts on the neighboring Moesia Provincia.

Dacia Provincia – later divided into smaller components – was in existence for barely more than 250 years. How significant is this period? What happened during this time, and what became of the Dacians? According to the Daco-Roman Continuity theory, the Romanian people, speaking the Neo-Latin language and forming a majority of the population living in present day Romania, are the direct descendants of the ethnic Dacians who became Romanized in the Dacia Provincia. The Dacians, conquered and submissive at the time of Trajan, quickly made Roman culture their own and remained in place after the withdrawal of Rome. Their descendants still live there and have moved but little with time.

As far as Romanization is concerned, the Romanians foster the concept by claiming that during the two great campaigns of Trajan, a substantial number of the Dacians offered no real resistance. This would explain the sudden collapse of the previously triumphant and clever Decebalus. They seem to have anticipated the new status and culture that Rome offered to those who submitted voluntarily in a new province. It was this surrender that created the opportunity to accept the blessings of the advanced Roman civilization, everything, in fact, that is subsumed by the single word, Romanization.

The counter-arguments are weighty. Trajan's troops had to fight long and bloody battles to make the establishment of Dacia Provincia possible. Furthermore, the Roman rule was never as complete and pervasive in Transylvania, where the geographic configurations favored the defenders, as it was in the gently rolling hill country of Pannonia. It is also possible that while the upper crusts of the Dacians, the "Fur Hat People" suffered severe losses during the fighting, the "Longhairs" became a Dacian subject people to the Romans. It is also possible that some of the Transylvanian mountain strongholds never came under Roman rule. These small spots survived Dacia Provincia, or, at least, a substantial portion of its existence.

The ethnic and spiritual Romanization, which must be assumed as an essential component of the Daco-Roman continuity theory, did not take place even where Roman sovereignty, hegemony and cultural influence were much stronger and where the local resistance was much weaker both initially and later – in Pannonia, for instance where, compared to Dacia, Roman rule lasted two to two and a half times as long and was maintained for almost half a millennium. The local Pannonian and Celt populations barely resisted the Romans initially, and later on, there were no outbreaks against the Roman rule, such as were fomented repeatedly by the Dacians in their own territory.

If we were writing the history of the Romanian people and of the Romanian "National State", we could list numerous arguments why so many Romanians should consider the Daco-Roman relations and the emphasis on continuity, so logical and indeed inevitable, both politically and psychologically. In addition, this theory is strengthened by the many Latin elements in the Romanian language. On the other hand, the precise findings provided by archeological excavations hardly serve to support the continuity hypothesis. Although psychologically weighty, this theory of national identity and occupation by "historic rights" is legally just as inconsequential, and worth exactly as little as the declarations on the Hungarian side which claim that the Carpathian basin is our "Hun inheritance" and that we had occupied it at the time of the Arpadian conquest as direct descendants of Attila's Huns.

Significant ethnic changes appeared early in Dacia Provincia. The fact that Roman veterans began to settle the land very rapidly, points to an optimistic attitude. The fact that large numbers of people moved in for the exploitation of the gold mines suggests that the precious metal supplies in Transylvania – in the absence of any data from the Dacian times – had again become a valuable asset. These new settlements, however, did not fulfill the earlier expectations. They did not bring peace to the area. The uprisings suggest that the complete pacification of the Dacians was not achieved in spite of the Romans' considerable military superiority. In fact, the area became even less secure for the Romans, particularly when internal uprisings coincided with attacks from the outside. Finally, in the middle of the third century, the Romans yielded Dacia to the Goths. This shortened their overly long border (*limes*) which was subject to numerous assaults and freed troops, very much in demand in other areas.

For us, the fate and problems of the Roman Empire, weighty though they may be, are of less interest. We are much more interested in those who – perhaps – stayed in place. Is it possible to assume a Daco-Roman Continuity on the basis of what we know about them? We will try to approach this problem from two sides. One is the appearance of the Neo-Latin people. This can be seen only within the original patrimony of the Roman Empire and even there only considerably later than the cession of Dacia. The second approach is more direct. It evaluates the local events on the basis of the changes that took place in Transylvania at that time and which can be properly documented.

The Roman withdrawal from Dacia was followed by a reasonably peaceful time. By then, however, wars and epidemics had made significant inroads into the local population. This made it possible for the departing Romans to take a major portion of the remaining inhabitants with them – primarily those most closely allied with them – and settle them within the boundaries of the new borders. The former Dacia was left as the spoils, battle ground and living space to the Goths, Carps, Sarmatians, Gepids and Vandals. The complete excavation of some contemporary cemeteries could irrevocably prove – or disprove – the continued survival of a "Romanized Dacian population". We know of no such excavation in contemporary Romania. It must be noted that in the Latin Dacian inscriptions we find that the majority of names are Oriental rather than Latin (Italian). Perhaps Christian inroads had already begun under the Roman rule. In Pannonia we have evidence of episcopal sees, shortly after the Roman occupation. Such evidence from Dacia is lacking. Even more damaging is the almost complete absence of place names of Latin origin in the area of present Transylvania. Rome is remembered only by the name of some rivers. (The recently introduced place names – e.g., Cluj-Napoca – have been revived artificially after an interval of almost 2000 years.)

What then was the fate of the Dacians? Those who remained in the old Dacia Provincia disappeared in the great melting pot of the great migrations. Those who moved toward the south and

southwest were assimilated by the hot-blooded people of the Balkans. After the dissolution of Dacia
Provincia, we hear practically nothing about contemporary Dacians during the following three to
four centuries. This is not at all surprising. Just the
opposite! Many people and ethnic groups of the
Great Migrations continued their biologic existence
only by giving up their former individuality. Their
units and groups lose their identity or rather gain a
new one. This is not their triumph or their shame;
this is as it should be in an orderly progression in
nature and history.

Then, if not descendants of the Dacians, who are
the Romanians? Whence and when did they come
and settle in the former lands of the Dacians – or, at
least, on part of that land? It is a much later story
which begins somewhere else and we will return to
it at the proper place and time.

The Period of the Great Migrations

*W*hen looking at Transylvania after the Romans left Dacia and before the Hungarians settled there – the former took place around 271 and the latter after 896 – it must be emphasized that just as Dacia Provincia did not cover the entire geographic unit referred to later as Transylvania, the changes in populations and governments described for these six centuries also did not affect the entire area of Transylvania, nor its entire population. Thus, the changes could be both consecutive and parallel. It is not possible, nor is it necessary, in this book to follow all these changes in detail either geographically or temporally.

We know of a brief Carp interlude but following this, the above mentioned Goth occupation was both widespread and long-lasting, so much so that the Visigoths were occasionally referred to as Sylvan Goths because of the settlement of this group in the forested parts of Transylvania. Contrary to their name, however, and to their reputation as nomads breeding large herds of cattle and horses, these people primarily settled in the most fertile parts of Transylvania, where they led an agricultural existence. They became familiar with Christianity, thanks to Arian missionaries.

When the Hun forces increased their drive toward the west, they first defeated the Ostrogoths and then destroyed the main forces of the Visigoth chieftain Athanaric (376). The remnants of the Visigoths first fled to their brethren in Transylvania, but later the entire Visigoth population sought the protection of Rome and, following the tracks of the Dacians, retreated behind the eastern boundaries of the Roman Empire.

The Goth period of Transylvania was a period of destruction. They didn't use the Roman buildings and allowed them to fall into decay. Their entire way of life – because or in spite of their agriculturist nature – was much simpler than what was typical of the earlier Dacia Provincia. Yet this was only the beginning of the decay that followed the departure of the Romans.

Before the Huns, responsible for the largest migrations of peoples of these times, could themselves take over the reign of this area, there was an interlude of several events associated with the Gepids. The Gepids who were blood relations of the Germanic Visigoths, were also eastern Germanic and came down from the region of the Vistula. The most noteworthy part of their rich archeological material is the famous Szilágysomlyó treasure. Its owners buried it and later lacked the opportunity of recovering it. From this we may speculate on the fate of the Gepid leadership during the times of the Huns and assume that this people had lost its entire ruling class, at least for a while.

During the decades between 420-450, certain parts of Transylvania – primarily along the Maros and in the valleys of the Southern Carpathians – with their cool forests rich in game, served the Hun leaders as summer quarters. Toward the north, the Gepids, under new leaders appointed by the Huns and subject to the Huns, gained new strength. Soon, their foot soldiers became the main and most important auxiliary force of the Hun forces and served under Attila all the way to the fateful battle of Catalaunum. This is a familiar scenario. The inner strength of a defeated people leads it to a new flowering in such a plastic and complex ethnic power structure as the Hun Empire and system. Ardaric, the king imposed upon the Gepids by the Huns, standing at the helm of the united armies of the peoples of the Danube basin just two years after Attila's death (453) gains victories against those who had elevated him to the kingship. The Gepid kingdom established and expanding after these events, ruled for more than a century over an area larger than Transylvania or the former Dacia Provincia. During this period, the Dacians and other splinter groups, who retreated behind the Roman borders, were forced to move further west-southwest from the Carpathians.

All this coincided with the Merovingian epoch in Europe. The name, originally that of a dynasty, also signifies a level of development which reached far beyond the actual realm of the Merovingians and which permeated all ways of life. What does this mean? It means primarily the reversal of the economic decline following the dissolution of the homogenous Roman civilization. It also means some improvements in productivity and a new form of urbanization. The center of this Merovingian development was ruled by the Franks and this central area extended in the west to the Atlantic. In the east, there was no sharp line of demarcation, but it extended in a wide arc over a peripheral area, easy to trace all the way to the former Pannonia. East of here the limits of the periphery extended all the way to the eastern end of Transylvania and demonstrated the indirect but characteristic effects of the Merovingian evolution. Beyond Transylvania this evolution, which had shaped much of Europe, did not have even an indirect effect. The newly independent Gepid Kingdom, which extended well beyond Transylvania to the center of the adjacent Great Plain created a century-long solid stability, which demonstrated to several generations the value of rapprochement and attachment to Europe. This is amply documented by the Gepid royal tombs from this period and by other graves rich in artifacts.

In the meantime, displaced from their original home in Central Asia and under pressure from the Turcic tribes, a new nation, capable of creating a dominant concentration of power, appeared on the scene. The Avars begin a fantastic "reel" around the Carpathian basin. They first appeared by the lower Danube, but when they found there neither an opportunity for settlement nor a possibility to proceed toward the south, they marched around the Carpathians to the north to the Elbe, where the Franks forced them back.

Subsequently, they tried again to establish a foothold, indeed we may say, a conquest along the lower Danube. Being again unsuccessful, they once again circled the Carpathians toward the north and penetrated as far as Thuringia. Here their path was blocked again by the Franks, but now the Franks offered an alliance. Not only their own, but also that of the Longobards allied with them.

It is of interest concerning these future founders of Lombardy in northern Italy, that their movements in our space are known "from minute to minute" – an occurrence extremely rare at this period. They arrived on the soil of Pannonia in 546 and they left for the south 22 years later, at Easter of 568. As late arrivals, they were initially adversaries of the Gepids. The latter were surrounded by enemies on all sides: Byzantium, the Slavs infiltrating from the north, the still wandering Avars, and now the Longobards, who had suddenly occupied the course of the Danube from the west. The fate of the Gepids was sealed but the people was even now not entirely exterminated. Its survival can be seen in a number of areas, but the Gepid kingdom was finished. Not much later the Gepid remnants were assimilated and disappeared.

The scenario is plain. The enemies of the Gepids "generously" offered the land of these people to the Avars. They killed two birds with one stone; they rid themselves of the warlike Gepids and offered the opportunity to settle down to the equally feared, bellicose Avars. It was from them that the Hungarians, even more feared at a future date, learned – still in Asia – the use of the stirrups. This enabled them to sit their horses much more securely, shoot their arrows more accurately, attack as a compact cavalry unit – and turn around and flee if necessary.

Trading Avars for Gepids? A dubious exchange. An already Europeanized nation was replaced in the heart of the easily defensible Carpathian basin by the Avars, fresh from Asia with Asiatic élan and Asiatic temperament. This was very much appreciated by the Longobards who, in spite of the jointly gained victory, immediately saw the advantages of departing from the Carpathian basin. Their departure was followed by an Avar suzerainty over this area, lasting almost a quarter of a millennium (567-827).

Initially, Transylvania had little appeal to the Avars, who were still engaged in a primarily Asiatic type of animal husbandry. They settled here in small numbers, leaving room to settle for the Slavs and for a series of subsequent Turcic waves. In this region the late Avar settlements and grave-sites, dating to the second half of the Avar Empire, are even rarer. Yet there is much uncertainty in all this, particularly in the history of the settlements. The excavations are sparse and their assessment is much influenced by all that is involved in the unfortunate Daco-Roman Continuity hypothesis. When the study of the ethnicity of a former population of a region and of their entire social structure is permeated, debated and distorted by politico-ideological considerations, the threads of historical assessment become hopelessly entangled.

We have already mentioned the slow, gradual "seepage", rather than invasion, of the Slavs into this region. This was directed initially southward, more toward the Balkans. The Slavs went from the north "toward the sun". When this progress was impeded, they encircled the Carpathians. It was only later that they penetrated into the Avar territory, principally across the wooded peripheral areas which had been very sparsely inhabited for many years. It was in these regions that they established their poor but tenacious and long-lasting settlements.

Vanishing Gepids, subject to the dominant Avars; agriculturist Slavs whose undemanding nature served them better then weapons; several small, fragmented groups; and finally in South Transylvania, beginning with the second quarter of the 9th century, an invading Bulgarian group – this was the colorful ethnic palette of this area toward the end of the 9th century. In the meantime, the powerful and previously dominant Avars were weakened more by their internal dissensions and fratricidal battles than by their external enemies. At this very moment, leaving the disintegrating Khazar Khanate just outside the Carpathians, a new nation approached, pressured by expansive, warlike nations behind them. They first galloped around the Carpathians and then over-ran the Carpathian basin and, just like the Avars, concentrated on the central, level area.

This is the first nation that could gain such a solid foothold here that the country established by them survives to this day. The movements of the Great Migration, mobilizing nation after nation, did not end with their arrival and settlement, not even with the organization of their state. The subsequent waves of the Great Migration harass them but can neither destroy them nor assimilate them, nor chase them off. All the territories around them are already firmly occupied. There is no place for them to go.

The Scourge of Europe

$\mathcal{W}$e are not familiar with the precise course of the Hungarian conquest. It is certain, however, that our ancestors were looking for a new home in an area previously already well known to them. During earlier, long range forays – exploratory and looting ventures – they repeatedly entered the Carpathian basin and even went beyond it. They were particularly familiar with the area between the Carpathians and the Black Sea, but they had visited the Balkans, the foothills of the Alps, the Vienna basin and Moravia. Their forays were undertaken either on their own or on invitation. In this region, the dissolution of the Avar Empire – according to newer information, as consequence of the ravages of an extensive draught – left a power vacuum which a number of groups tried to fill. These groups were situated around the periphery and intermittently either fought or formed alliances with each other. They were frequently looking for "military adventurers" who could be hired for money or for other considerations.

According to the simplest version of the history of our conquest, the seven Hungarian tribes were forced out from their former home in the Etelköz (between rivers) and were joined by the Kabars who had come from the Khazar Khanate. They supposedly crossed the northern passes of the Carpathians, but perhaps only the Verecke pass. This theory seems to be strongly supported by the fact that the area just below the Verecke pass, the Zemplén-Szabolcs region, is particularly rich in graves dating to the period of the conquest. Furthermore, we can be reasonably certain that some of the graves excavated in the cemetery at Karos in the Bodrogköz, are the only ones which held the bodies of men who were in the original conquest group and who were still born beyond the Carpathians in the Etelköz.

Later, another theory became acceptable, according to which the invasion came from two directions, from Verecke and from the lower Danube, thus both from the north and also from the south. Today we believe that the majority of the conquering groups entered their new homeland through the passes of the eastern Carpathians. In both of the latter cases, in addition to Zemplén and Szabolcs, Transylvania was among the first regions to be settled. Soon thereafter, the conquering Hungarians expanded rapidly toward the west in the Felvidék, the present-day Slovakia, while the subjugation of Pannonia took place only several years later. All in all, the Hungarian conquest began in 895 and was completed in 900. During this time and for another 70 years thereafter, the Hungarians still engaged in military adventures.

At this time, and for a long period of time, Europe was under a threefold pressure. In the south, from

Africa, the Moors (Arabs) tried to establish themselves in or at least gather rich plunder from Iberia and Italy. In the north, the fast ships of the Vikings (Normans) circled the Continent and attacked from the south and from the north. They didn't care whether the water under their keels was salt or sweet, sea or river. In the center the wild Hungarians rampaged over an enormous area. The hooves of their horses splashed in the waters of the Baltic in the north, and of the Channel in the west. In the southwest they reached the center of Iberia and in the south they looked across the narrows to Sicily. In Greece only the Peloponesus remained inviolate and in the east only the Bosporus stopped them. Europe was slow to react. It was much more important to the European nations to fight over the detached remnants of the former Roman Empire than to unite to curtail these three bellicose people.

In spite of their repeated and long-lasting conquests, the Moors were eventually forced out of Europe and had to withdraw to Africa, which brought little joy to the resident African tribes. Those branches of the Vikings who settled far from their original Scandinavian home later participated in the formation of the Russian state, gave their name to Normandy and established a Norman kingdom in Sicily. All this at the price, however, that the few remaining groups ultimately were assimilated into the larger mass of the people conquered and organized by them.

The Hungarians, on the other hand, took solid control of their new home in the Carpathian basin.

Very soon they could establish a state that was ethnically quite colorful but which was made cohesive by the language spoken being Hungarian.

These three groups, who originated from far distant regions and whose goals and aims differed widely, still served a common purpose. By being a threat to all the nations of Europe and to the entire power structure of the Continent, they hastened the reversal of the chaotic fragmentation that followed the fall of the Roman Empire. Involuntarily of course, but they were instrumental in triggering the formation of the administrative bases and borders which have changed many times over the past thousand years, but which even then drew an ethnic and national outline or sketch map of Europe very much as it is today.

In the second half of the 9th century, the Hungarian forays could no longer be maintained with the same enthusiasm and they slowly came to a complete stop. It was not the bellicose spirit that was lacking. It was their paymasters, the European monarchs and pretenders using their services, who slowly came to their senses. Politically, they realized that if they weakened their neighbors and their neighbors' economy by the depredations of the mercenary Hungarians, they would all suffer in the end. They also realized that the Hungarian light cavalry tactics could be opposed successfully. Responding to a ruse with a ruse they gave up responding piecemeal and city by city. They appreciated that by joining forces, this voracious people driving a wedge into the heart of Europe could be stopped. At the same time, the wiser Hungarian tribal or tribal alliance leaders realized that their foes whom they despoiled or whose money they earned with their blood had come to their senses. This realization was bilateral and mutually effective.

The restless, sanguinary Hungarians must be forced into the ranks of the Christian European nations, living within secure borders, or they must be destroyed. We must become a part of the predominantly Christian Europe or we will be exterminated. Since it is difficult to determine the accurate course of the Hungarian conquest, it follows that the history of the conquest of Transylvania also lacks precision. The more so since the Romanian national prejudice makes the continuation of archeological excavations difficult and interferes with the publication and judicious interpretation of the findings. If, however, we accept the last of the conquest theories discussed above, or if we were to completely discard the northern or Verecke theory, as some historians have, then the dominant majority of the conquerors must have reached Transylvania in the first phase of the conquest. Most of them could not remain there, since this region could not support them and their animals. The majority had to move rapidly to the more fertile parts of the Carpathian basin and to an area more suited for a pastoral economy.

The group of conquerors remaining in Transylvania gathered in the central region, mainly along the upper tributaries of the Maros and the Szamos. Even though initially the Bulgarian neighbors were important, very soon Byzantium became the dominant power factor, and it was natural that the Eastern Christian Church should have cast its rays upon Transylvania.

Originally Byzantium was not a target for Hungarian adventurers. They lived in alliance with it, or took tribute (peace ransom) from it. Even later, when the Eastern Empire came under attack by them, the loot gathered there was found by the archaeologists not in Transylvania, but along the Tisza, in the graves of the former marauders. Could it be that the Hungarians living in Transylvania at that time did not join the adventurers assaulting Byzantium? This suggests a certain autonomy. Was there such a thing and what was it based on? Investigation of this matter is made difficult by the fact that following the conquest, and at the time of the adventuring as well as immediately thereafter, there were two converging processes going on in Hungarian society, in its power structure and later in the territorial arrangements of its people. Before and during the conquest, the tribal separation was still pronounced, but now – largely under Árpád's influence – the tribes became increasingly united and combined into a tribal confederacy. Increasingly, but not entirely. The adventuring was in part certainly a tribal undertaking or the "private affairs" of two or more jointly acting tribes. The tribal confederacy dealt only with important matters affecting the entire nation. At the same time the confederation – ducal? princely? – had a dual power structure. The real leader was known as the *gyula,* while the spiritual leader was the *kende.*

The most likely version is that the confederacy of the conquerors was organized, still in the Etelköz, by Álmos, and that both he and his son Árpád held the dignity of the gyulaship. During the conquest, the aged Álmos was killed in Transylvania or on Transylvania's borders. It was written that "he was not to reach Pannonia". He became the victim of a ritual regicide. Was it because the people were forced to leave their original home? Or was it to celebrate the successful conquest? Or was it simply because his term of office had expired and because the time allotted for his supreme command was over? According to one hypothesis, this time period was nineteen years which, according to the Metón cycle of the calendar, corresponds to one lunar year.

At this time, the office of *kende* was held by Kurszán, who also shortly became a victim of murder. He was killed treacherously, during a conference, at the dinner table, by the Bavarians. This is noteworthy since with the death of Kurszán, the dual principality came to an end, even though its memory persisted and exerted a strong, traditional, retrospective attraction. There were attempts to re-establish it. The first and principal indication for this is that – primarily in Transylvania – there was after Árpád a whole series of anonymous rulers during whose rule a dynasty of "gyulas" appeared, who naturally also came from the ruling family. This regional dynasty tried to establish a balance of power vis-à-vis the Hungarian centrum, looked toward Byzantium, and converted to Eastern Christianity. It is not clear just how, but the title *gyula* later on becomes Gyula, i.e. a personal name. Could this be the result of historiography which transposes a title into a name?

When at the end of the 10th century the adventuring came to an end, the name of Géza emerges clearly and unmistakably from the chaotic and perhaps fictional list of princely names. Géza played a major role in numerous matters which heretofore were attributed exclusively to (Saint) Stephen I, who is venerated as the founder of the country. He – or perhaps his father – looked for a mate of dynastic interest. The one he married was called by the pagan-sounding name of Sarolt (white stoat, lady stoat or, more commonly, ermine). The father of the bride kept a princely court in the Transylvanian Fehérvár, which later became known as Gyula-fehérvár. The *gyula*, very powerful in Transylvania, may have been induced to accept Géza as his son-in-law because in the middle of the 970s the always powerful and dangerous Bulgarians became even more so, and managed to isolate him territorially from Byzantium. Later, Byzantium became stronger again, but at this time, in view of Géza's age, the reins of government were grasped by the energetic Sarolt. The relative independence of Transylvania was maintained under Sarolt's younger brother – another *gyula* – and this blood relationship served to provide security for both areas. Stephen, who became Prince in 1000 and was crowned king in 1001, was not satisfied with this arrangement. He married a Bavarian princess, and what Géza could accomplish with his marriage, his son, who married westward, had to accomplish with the force of arms.

First, he had to overcome Koppány in Somogy, though not because he was a pagan, and certainly not more than a partial pagan, like Géza.

The archaeologists have discovered the same type of four-apsed chapel in Bakonykoppány that was unearthed in Stephen's royal city of Székesfehérvár. It was not a religious difference that made Stephen confront Koppány, but the overthrow of the seniority-based succession that was characteristic of the Árpád dynasty in earlier times. After Géza's death, the Somogy magnate demanded the hand of the widowed Sarolt, along with the throne. After his overthrow, he was quartered and one of his quarters was nailed to the gate of Gyulafehérvár as an overt warning. This being insufficient, Stephen had to take an army against his maternal uncle. Subsequently, Stephen had to settle with another Transylvanian magnate, Ajtony, who became too independent and who had been known to "divert" the royal salt barges. Both of these campaigns are now viewed as though Gyula and Ajtony had already acted on behalf of non-Hungarian ethnic groups, Protodacians or Preromanians, and for independence from the new ambitious kingdom.

Actually, both of these campaigns were internal – Hungarian "family fights" for power. The uncertainty or absence of sources makes it impossible to date Stephen's campaign against Ajtony with any precision. Yet the complete incorporation of Transylvania into the administrative and religious structure created by Stephen could have taken place only subsequent to it.

Alternating historical and archeological approaches, we must emphasize that from the conquest to the creation of the State, the Hungarian presence in Transylvania does not imply that a small ruling class of Hungarians had been imposed on the local population. The frequently hampered and incomplete archeological studies document the presence of a large number of lower class Hungarian settlers.

Rex and Dux,
Mines and Border Guards

After Stephen strengthened both his position and the position of his central administrative base, he systematically proceeded to consolidate the smaller, and thus individually hardly threatening counties, which he then entrusted to his followers. He also established a network of bishoprics which covered the entire country and endowed a number of monasteries and chapters. This naturally extended to Transylvania as well. Here, however, a precise reconstruction is made difficult, among other reasons, by a delay in written documentation and by the fact that the numerous wars and internal uprisings seriously damaged the religious depositories of these documents. Thus, the medieval material of the archives gives only incomplete information or even misinformation, since the "earliest" documents that have come down to us are not truly the earliest documents pertaining to these sites, but only the earliest that we have been able to discover.

It is certain, however, that the organization of counties in Transylvania followed a definite pattern, and that these territorial-administrative-economic units were designed in this area with the defense of the kingdom as the paramount consideration.

Namely, the Transylvanian counties at this time did not have a defined border toward the "outside", in the direction of the Carpathians and the castles serving as the administrative centers were established on their most secure, western segment of the counties. While the counties and bishoprics – among them the Csanád bishopric, which was headed by the tutor of the Crown Prince Imre, the later martyr and saint, Gellért – were the products and depositories of a strong, central will, there emerged a fateful counter-current, which we may refer to as the trend toward regional constitutional laws. Parenthetically: if we accept the etymology of the name Erdély (Transylvania) – and why shouldn't we? – namely: Erdőelve = Beyond the Forest (literally Trans-Sylvania), we must know that it was the central mountains of Erdély, the Bihar Mountains, that were covered with huge, dense forests beyond which, according to contemporary thinking, Erdély (Transylvania) was located.

Stephen, having defeated Koppány, and having warded off Gyula's forceful and Ajtony's less significant endeavors toward independence, was looking farther into the future. In order to increase the legitimacy of his son Imre, to guide him into the arduous profession of ruling, and to give him a taste of its reality, he used not only the Admonitions – attributed to him but actually only inspired by him, but he also used the promising crown prince as an important war leader and, in fact, promoted him to a viceregal position. Thus, Emericus Dux, appointed by Stephanus Rex, was entrusted with Bihar, between the eastern border of the Great Plain and the western border of Transylvania, as a quasi autonomous realm. The new State thus evolved a dual administrative-economic axis, the first one between Esztergom and Székesfehérvár, which could be extended toward Pécs, the other one between Biharvár and Csanádvár, the northern pole of which was transferred shortly to Nagyvárad.

When Prince Imre was killed in a hunting accident in Bihar, probably along the upper reaches of the Berettyó, during a boar hunt, Stephen's hopes for a secure succession were lost. What remained was a dubious precedent, which was not unusual at this time and which was also familiar in Hungarian traditions. This was the institution of the *ducatus* (dukedom). Later, during the reign of the House of Árpád, this promising office was usually entrusted to the younger brother of the reigning king, who was then ready and waiting for the time when he could legally take the single, legal step toward the throne.

During the 11th century, a number of Petcheneg attacks reached Transylvania through the eastern passes of the Carpathians, and some of these attacks extended to the Great Plain. It became apparent that the traditional Hungarian system of the buffer zone with a wide, uninhabited area separating it from the neighboring people and countries failed to provide adequate protection, even though the defenders of this buffer zone were supposed to halt the first assault of the enemies, and even though there were defensive lines with one earthen defensive castle in every county. For this reason, additional castles were built according to a plan that would be called today "a defense in depth".

As far as the history of the settlements and of the ethnic mix of the population is concerned, the picture of the first centuries of Transylvania under Hungarian rule can be determined from the names of the settlements and of the rivers. This nomenclature, which persisted even during the subsequent settlements by Saxons and Romanians, with some modification according to their language, uniformly attests that in the 9th and 10th centuries this region was shared by the remnants of the earlier Slavic population and the conquering Hungarians, in the most part well separated from each other. This arrangement was possible because the older Slavic population preferred, for reasons of defense, the heavily forested areas, while the lately arrived Hungarians settled in the valleys and basins more suitable for grazing and for agriculture.

No organic continuity can be demonstrated for the towns or larger settlements of the former Dacia Provincia. Sometimes even the simplest signs of life are missing in the ruins which have lain uninhabited for centuries. Their names are forgotten. They are recalled only by the enthusiasm of recent times, but initially the impetus is not the Daco-Roman Continuity hypothesis. It is due rather to the currently popular and nostalgic retrospection to times long past and to antiquity. Neo-Latin was an earlier product of the love of Antiquity of its devotees. It was only later that it fit in well with the romantic, vigorous, national aspirations of the Romanians, and was most suitable to their ideology and rationalizations.

During the reign of Stephen and of his first successors, the social structure of Transylvania showed no difference from that of the country in general. The stratification, the rule and the subservience evolved in the same fashion as on "this side of the forest".

Why, and to what extent did this new East-Central European country, the Hungarian kingdom, need this province, which extended far to the east, and which differed from every other province by its natural geography? It is fundamental in this regard that those who rushed hither from the Etelköz saw the entire Carpathian basin as a unit which suited their way of life and which provided their desperately desired security. It is characteristic that they very soon relinquished the Viennese basin, which they also conquered as far as the present Melk, when they realized that it was a poorly defensible western salient. The correctness of their assessment is shown by the fact that the realm, lasting from the conquest to the 20th century, was interrupted for any length of time only twice. The Turks entered through the soft underbelly along the lower Danube, while the Germans (Austrians) entered along the upper Danube, from the Viennese basin.

Salt was the economically most important product of medieval Transylvania. Its commercialization and distribution was facilitated by the fact that its bulk could be transported by water, mostly on the Tisza and its tributaries, but also on the Maros network, which was a part of the Tisza network, but was important enough to merit special attention. Even though Hungary had century-long access to the Adriatic, the production of salt by evaporating sea water was more difficult and its transport more cumbersome than mining the salt deposits of the ancient seas and distributing of large blocks of rock salt.

Even though the data do not reflect it, it seems very unlikely that the mining of the previously so important Transylvanian precious metals was not continued under Stephen and under his first successors. It is also clear that a significant number of furs and raw hides were obtained from this region. One part of the very large herd of horses must also have served for export. It was this that stimulated the rapaciousness of the occasional invaders.

We had some kings whose activities and legends are characteristically related to a certain part of the country. Ladislas I, who was successful in arranging the canonization of Stephen, Imre and some others of his favorites, and who later was himself elevated to the gallery of Hungarian saints, according to legend, performed most of his great and miraculous deeds in Transylvania. The best known of these, also known as the St. Ladislas Legend, is a variation on the theme of his chivalrous deeds and relates how the king saved the daughter of the bishop of Várad from a marauding Cumanian fighter. This legend, which is depicted most frequently in Transylvanian churches – oddly enough, mostly in the mining communities – has an additional piquancy. It is not bad enough that the legend is full of pagan motives and allusions not quite becoming to a sainted king, but, that after the fight, the maiden saved from the Cumanian, "looked into the head" of the victorious knight, i.e. picked off the lice. This motif is disturbing not only because from today's perspective it is distressing that the knightly king, the future saint, had headlice, but also because such an intimate, personal activity by the maiden could have been performed only to her lover, a man who, speaking biblically, "had known her".

Returning to earth from the sphere of legends, it is certain that Ladislas I extended the borders of Transylvania to the east and settled a privileged class of border guards in Transylvania with the charge of protecting the internal foothills of the Carpathians against the bellicose tribes, firmly settled on the eastern slopes of the Carpathians and usually identified with the Cumanians. It seems likely that it was this group of soldiers, with whom he must have had frequent contact in the course of his numerous campaigns, who created his circle of legends and spread the word about his miraculous deeds, usually associated with military activities. It may also have been due to them that when their patron died during the summer of 1095, he was first buried in Somogyvár, but his remains where soon transferred to Nagyvárad.

Even though a small number of Petchenegs participated in the protection of the borders on the principle that the robbers make the best thief catchers, Ladislas also recruited his own bow and arrow cavalry from other parts of the country, and thus a large number of Hungarians joined those of their compatriots who remained in place immediately after the conquest. They were Hungarians, but they were not yet Székelys.

At this time, the internal organization and legal status of the Transylvanian counties were not in any way special. The counties and religious organizations followed the same pattern as in the other parts of the country. The one thing that should be noted is that when Ladislas's successor, King Koloman, brought Croatia under his rule he sent a voivode to take charge. This Slavic position of honor, previously unknown in our country, did affect Transylvania fairly soon and certainly from the end of the 12th century. It will cause many political problems and, later, will create even more problems for the recording historians.

The voivode specially appointed over a larger region could enjoy much more power, or could grasp more power than the *ispán*s (*comes*) in charge of the smaller, individual counties. The temptation was great for the representative of the central authority to further his own ambitions at the expense of the regional interests. The voivodes frequently became rebellious little kings. On the other hand, in the case of the newly acquired Croatia, this form of legal administration was appropriate, if for no other reason, than for the pacification of the local southern Slavic people and of their leadership and reassurance that in this way they may have a certain amount of autonomy. In the case of Transylvania, it has led to the assumption that there was such an independence of the region and of its people. For this there is no evidence and no precedent in the objective study of the 10th and 11th centuries. If there was any such independence, it was much earlier, at the time of the *gyula*s, and certainly no later than the time of Ajtony.

How Does it Happen that Three is Really Four?

As mentioned in the Prologue, one of the historic, and not geographic, characteristics of Transylvania was its specific population. Even at the earliest mention of them, they were already a Hungarian speaking people, and yet they were the clearly distinctive Székelys. They considered themselves to be the descendants of the army of Csaba, one of Attila's sons, who returned to Transylvania along the Highway of the Armies – the heavenly Milky Way. They thus considered themselves to be Hun in origin. This is one of the world-wide Savior myths, in which the divine liberator is not some placid prophet who can be crucified, but a belligerent leader of armies. The origin and prehistory of the Székelys are lost in obscurity, or rather there are so many hypotheses concerning them, that both the interested layman and the inquisitive expert are overtaken by dizziness. It has been mentioned repeatedly, but without any evidence, that the Hungarians already found them in the Carpathian basin in 895. Their archaic organization clearly points to Asiatic Turcic traditions strengthened by the long-time survival of Turcic runic script among them, yet the Székely dialect shows no deviation whatever from the Hungarian as far as the occurrence and prevalence of Finno-Ugrian, Turcic or other linguistic remnants is concerned. It is a fact that in the campaigns of the Árpád era, they had to serve both as scouts and as rearguard. This suggests a recent contact, since the dangers and bloody losses ensuing from these assignments were always imposed by the military rulers of the nomadic peoples on their latest allies or subjects.

The least controversial theory of their origin suggests that the Székelys were remnants of the Kabars who joined the Hungarians at the time of the dissolution of the Khazar Khanate, when the perhaps forcefully ejected Hungarians started out to find a new homeland. It is certain that they were not scattered, or at least not scattered as much as the seven conquering Hungarian tribes during the postnomadic period, when Hungarian society was transformed and reshaped by the strength and the demands of the centralized royal power.

They became guardians of the borders. They were not the first ones and not the last ones. Yet, they served in this capacity for such a long time, and with such lasting effects on the life of numerous generations, as was unprecedented among the Hungarians in the Carpathian basin.

In Transylvania, in the Székelyföld (Land of the Székelys), a large and tightly knit block emerged. In the other borderlands of the country, thus principally in the southwestern part of Transdanubia, the Göcsej, north of Pozsony and in the Bihar, the individuality of the small Székely groups, their autonomy and characteristics rapidly started to disintegrate, fade and disappear. Next to Transylvania, the most persistent traces come from Göcsej, but among the people in this region only the faintest folkloric traditions testify to their original provenance.

The basic population was divided into six clans which, in turn, were sub-divided into four branches each, and thus gave structure to society, to the family and to the economic and military existence of the nation. The judges who saw to their affairs and their leaders in war were designated so that inheritance, election, recall and rotation all played a role. In such a system, there was considerable rigidity but also not a little flexibility.

When the Transylvanian Székely "szék"-s were established – *szék* in this context means a territorial and administrative unit and, incidentally, is totally unrelated to the name of the people – the societal structure of these units duplicated and reflected the national whole. They did not move or settle by clans or by branches if such a move was forced upon them, but always in almost random groupings assembled from the entire nation. This was carried to the point that when some major disaster reduced or destroyed a branch, the area was reconstituted and replenished from the other branches in order to maintain the continuity of tradition.

For a long time, the Székelys kept to simple animal husbandry and to a grazing economy with a nomadic changing of their pastures. The forests and the land were owned jointly. The families had the right to use the land but had no right of ownership.

Even later, when private ownership became stronger, a sensible collectivism was stubbornly maintained with a village-based joint ownership and with the repeated opportunity to redistribute joint property according to need. Yet, they could not remain untouched by their feudal environment, and there was also an ongoing internal differentiation. Thus, a Székely nobility evolved on an economic basis. The rest of the population was divided into those who fought on horseback and those who fought "only" on foot, thus forming the three classes identified clearly both in peace at home and in war. The Székelys gained their privileges and independence with their own blood and toil. These were frequently threatened and the Székelys had to stand up again and again in their defense. They protested verbally, in writing and, occasionally, by taking up arms. This will be discussed later. Let us now return to the fateful history of the original settling of the land.

During the first third of our millennium much was already decided in a most ominous fashion. There are few written sources for fixing the years of their beginning. It can, however, be determined from indirect sources that the first Székely settlements in Transylvania took place during the reign of the first kings of the House of Árpád. When, during the reign of Géza II (1141-1162), in the middle of the 12th century, large scale German colonization took place which was going to have effects lasting nearly a millennium, the Germans settled in areas from where the border-guarding Székelys had been moved out, to be closer to the actual frontiers.

German colonization? In Transylvania, this group, traditionally strong in numbers, wealth and intellect, underwent a fateful decline only toward the middle of the 20th century. We refer to this German speaking population as the Saxons, just as we do to the related population in today's Slovakia, the former Hungarian Felvidék, and Upper Hungary. In contrast, the also German speaking groups who were settled in western and southern Transdanubia, in the southern Great Plain – mostly in the segment belonging to Serbia, where they formed an almost continuous ring – in a semicircle around Buda, and who also lived and live in decreasing numbers in scattered locations throughout the rest of the country, were called in the common parlance the Svabians.

A significant percentage of the "Saxons" are ethnically truly of Saxonian origin. Of our "Svabians" only a small fraction came originally from Svabia. In both groups there was a significant influx of many other ethnic German groups during the Middle Ages, as well as in more recent times. It is almost a historic accident that because of the ethnic origin of a few leading families, these two categories of Germans became a rigid fixture in the Carpathian basin and retained their designation in a dual and parallel fashion, assimilating subsequent and different German ethnic groups.

Transylvania became familiar with the county system. Then the Crown relegated Transylvania, or rather a part of Transylvania, to the authority of a voivode, the holder of which title stood between the counties and the central administration. The autonomy of the

Székelys survived in the *széks* or seats, where they were gathered into territorial and ethnic blocks. The arriving Saxons, whose first waves originated in and around Luxembourg and who left there to escape the rigid, feudal shackles, were also organized into *széks* and thus gained special opportunities and an autonomous administration. They also did not have to adapt themselves to the county system.

Later on, a Székely *ispán* was appointed. For a while, however, the Székely and Saxon *széks* were withdrawn from the voivode's authority and were combined under the control of the Szeben *ispán*. At this time – we are in 1210 – a source mentioned the Szeben *ispán* as the one who led the Székelys, the Saxons, the Petchenegs and the Romanians in war. The emphasis here is distinctly on the latter. Shortly before this time, the Pechenegs still attacked several times across the eastern Carpathians. The earlier Székely settlements were established largely for this reason. Later the Petchenegs became satellites, "robbers into thief catchers", and guardians of the borders. Their small numbers hastened their assimilation. We are not concerned with them here, but must mention, however, that it was not they who represent the fourth element in medieval Transylvania which appeared last, or perhaps simultaneously with the Saxons, and which joined the other communities induced or forced by circumstances into a lasting union.

Let us list the four: Hungarians, Székelys, Saxons and Romanians. The list is not weighted in any way and represents only the historic sequence. It is an open question why we are separating the Hungarians and the Székely into separate "nations" when they spoke the same language and who, according to one view, differed from each other but very slightly. This may even lead us into the camp of those who, for whatever reason, wished to decrease the demographic and historic role of the Hungarian presence in this region (hypothesizing even that the Székelys are Hungarianized Romanians). The answer is that the Székelys who were very proud, liked to consider themselves as a separate "nation", particularly when they hoped that this separateness would assure them their privileges as guardians of the borders, their Székely freedom and the autonomy inherent in their *széks*. A Székely "nation" is not a fiction, but has to be interpreted in the context of the times and of the prevalent legal concepts. The concept had a different meaning than what it has today. It meant a tribe or a tribal association – that is, a community of shared obligations, rights, duties and possibilities.

The predecessors of the early-latter day Romanians, who established their country late, but very successfully, were living at the time of the Hungarian conquest in the Central Balkans, where they were in close linguistic proximity with the Albanians who remained much closer to their original region. Linguistic evidence also suggests that most of them engaged in a pastoral life in the mountains. Since at that time this very hard life had little appeal, the higher mountainous regions gave them ample opportunities for expansion. In the early sources, Byzantium, a major power fighting a desperate defensive war at this time, called them the Wallachians, and it was only in the last century that this term became the pejorative designation of Oláh. The Byzantians actually called all the latinizing, non-Greek Balkanian people Wallachians, and were pleased to use the people so designated for their own purposes. The region was recognized as a desirable area during an almost incidental campaign – note how the Hungarians discovered the Carpathian basin during their first Central European incursion, and the idea of establishing a permanent residence here had considerable appeal.

We can find the first indications of an approach of the Wallachians from the external slopes of the Carpathians toward the Hungarian territory during the Byzantian campaign involving Transylvania in 1166. These dates – the Byzantian campaign of 1166 and the campaign of the Szeben *ispán* in 1210, using Wallachian fighters (actually against the Bulgarians and not the Byzantines) – determine the time when we can definitely assert that there was a Romanian ethnic presence on the soil of Transylvania. Their gaining strength was contributed to markedly by one of the greatest Hungarian historical cataclysms. But first an interlude.

There was already an organized German colonization in Transylvania, on territory formerly inhabited by the Székelys, when other, Germanic newcomers appeared, this time from the east. The Teutonic Knightly Order, authorized by a Papal Bull of 1198, had barely been established by German nobles in Palestine from among the knightly crusaders, when they were expelled from the Holy Land. They were chased back to Europe, and in 1211 the benevolent Andrew II (1205-1235) invited them to the Barcaság, mainly in order for them to oppose the Cumanian attacks and to convert the Cumanians, which truly was their mission. The Teutonic Order, which later proved to be so aggressive, very soon attempted to establish an independent country on the land received from us and to place themselves under the protection of the distant Pope and thus free themselves from the nearby Hungarian king. When after a number of ominous signals Andrew discovered that instead of the wooden castles, which he had very hesitantly approved, the Teutonic Knights were beginning to build permanent stone castles, the disappointed king expels them in 1225 by force of arms. Fleeing from Palestine, the Teutonic Order – after the brief interlude of their Transylvanian settlement – were issued a later much regretted invitation by the Poles and settled in Prussia and along the Baltic littoral. We will not follow their adventurous and, for so many, tragic and painful history.

Returning to the Romanians, Wallachians – the first charter which mentions them relates to the land of a Romanian village chief, in the Szörénység, and is dated 1247. They were primarily engaged in sheep and goat grazing, but as a consequence of their migratory way of life, they also bred horses and inhabited almost all habitable parts of a very wide area, north of Macedonia and south of Moldavia. Thus, to find the precise location of their original home is even more hopeless than it is for the Hungarians. For centuries, their main characteristic was migration, during which they lived and moved among a number of different ethnic groups. They participated in markets and, with their animals functioned as highly regarded carters and transporters. Wherever they were, they participated in local activities but the looseness of their affiliations satisfied their needs of the time. It did not, however, promote the concentration of the population needed for the formation of a country. It did maintain a way of life with a number of archaic traits. This initial dilatoriness, which was not rare at the turn of the millennium, was maintained by them for many-many generations.

Their coherence was strengthened by their religion. Examined in more detail, the animal husbandry which was pervasive among the Wallachians, albeit by no means exclusive to them, is hard to compress into the neat categories drawn up by the economic historians and ethnographers. A few definitions become unavoidable: in a nomadic system, the change of pasture – primarily the change between summer and winter pastures – involves the migration of the entire population. When only the shepherds accompany the flocks to the winter pastures, it is known as transhumation. This may have meant a trip of several hundred kilometers, twice each year and also forced the men into lengthy absences from their families. It had enormous effects on sexual customs and on the raising of children. In high altitude grazing, the flock grazed during the summer in the lush mountain meadows, and in the winter lived in stables on forage gathered during the summer. In these cases, the pasture and the home were usually not too distant from each other, and family life was not subject to a seasonal periodicity.

Depending on the region and the period, these three methods of animal husbandry were used interchangeably by the Wallachians. A description – admittedly from the last century – is so singularly affective that I must quote it. It describes the existence of a fourth method. Thus, "the life of these herdsmen is very singular and quite different from that of any other shepherd. With 60-70 of their master's goats they roam over the bare crags all winter. Completely left to their own devices, they are far from any social contacts and may not see another human being for months. In previously designated spots, such as caves or hollow trees, their master will have deposited cornmeal for them which the shepherds use as they go along. There is no variety in their days, they pass in complete uniformity. Such a shepherd picks a large beech tree and fells it in such a fashion that it falls unto one or two other beeches and thus bring down three trees at the same time. The more the better. His work takes several hours during which the goats watch from a safe distance, chew their cud and wait for their meal being prepared. When the centuries old beech trees hit the ground, the shepherd gives a yell and the hungry herd strips the buds and bark with their sharp teeth. The shepherd, having removed the snow, builds a huge fire and filling a large kettle with snow hangs it on a metal tripod. When the water boils, he adds cornmeal from his shoulder bag, stirs it into a porridge and dines as contentedly as the city dweller at a six course dinner. He slakes his thirst with the snow melted in his kettle and stretching out on a pile of branches sleeps soundly, having been awake all night for fear of predators. After the goats have consumed their dinner, they lie down but the shepherd soon interrupts their rest. He breaks a path through the deep snow and the goats follow in single file and so they go down into a valley where they spend the night, protected from the howling winds. He does not close his eyes all night and building several small fires around the herd to keep away the slavering wild animals, watches them until the morning. Should it start snowing again at night, the shepherd immediately rousts the herd from its rest and keeps them moving back and forth. Thus, they stamp the snow down, keep warm and also keep from being covered by snow. This is the daily routine of the mountain goat herd. Finally, after six months of misery, hard even to imagine for a person used to social intercourse, with a face blackened by storms and freezing cold, but with a sound, healthy stomach and in good strength he descends with his herd to the village."

I quoted from: "Sándor Ujfalvi, the old Hunter. Kolozsvár in the year 1854". I did this not only to show a new, albeit rather extreme form of animal husbandry; the quote says more about the incredible tenacity and simplicity shown by the men engaged in this form of animal care, who lived among their animals which, in turn, survived on buds and bark. This adaptability and the willingness to live like this were major factors in their entry into and expansion within the Balkans and the Carpathian basin. This was a vastly different approach than that of the other nations – including the Hungarians – who brought their cattle and horse breeding practices and their warlike traditions with them from the steppes of Asia.

In the region where the Wallachians lived and moved for a long time as transients, Romanianization was much stronger than in Transylvania and in Transylvanian Dacia. This was the area where the Proto-Romanians – under strong Slavic and other influences – became Latinized in their language and in the demonstrable orientation of their leading classes. They evidently also mingled, here and there, with the descendants of the early Dacians. This is a much more defensible hypothesis than that of the local Transylvanian continuity.

Their Latinity, while clearly dominant as far as their language is concerned, did not prove to be very strong in a much more important area. Initially, they were under the aegis of Christianity, following the Latin ritual. But the proximity of Byzantium, and perhaps under the influence of the Slavic people, they soon and irrevocably fell under the dominance of the Eastern Ritual. The Greek Orthodox Church, the Pravoslavia, never shaken by the Reformation that hit its Western counterpart, solidly permeated the entire social structure. Through religious instruction, philosophy and mentality it became a decisive factor for entire regions and people. Even today, the dividing line in the Balkans and in the Carpathian basin is not geographic or historic, but religious. It is the line between the Roman and the Eastern rites that separates Central Europe from Eastern Europe.

Gothic Spires and Onion Domes
Coming to the end of this chapter, we arrive in the middle of the 13th century. At this time, there were only two Transcarpathian events which affected the Wallachians and which deserve attention. For a short time, there was a Bulgarian-Wallachian state, and this was significant since it meant that the Wallachians, this Proto-Romanian ethnic group, began to participate in a higher order of organization than previously. Secondly, the Cumanians, whose proximity was the reason for the invitation to the Teutonic Order, also began to develop a more advanced administrative structure in the area to the east and to the south of the Carpathians. The Cumanians were transiently allied to the Bulgarian-Wallachian block, mentioned above, but the increasing pressure by the Tatars (Mongolians) from the East, made them look for assistance to the West and even accepted Christianity.

When Andrew II crowned his eight-year-old son Béla, the later Béla IV, as associate king – remember, there was a precedent for this – he gave him Transylvania as a "practice kingdom". When Béla reached adulthood, one of his main concerns was to attach Cumania to Hungary. In this he was eventually successful. By the time it was accomplished, however, a significant part of the Cumanian population became Wallachian. A basic area began to take shape, extending from the Havasalföld to Moldavia, where there were first Romanian voivodates, later Romanian principalities and finally – much later – the present Romanian fatherland. Young King Béla's conquests in the direction of Cumania were so successful that Hungarians, Székelys and Saxons in large numbers, voluntarily or otherwise, migrated to the region beyond the Carpathians. It is at this time that the ancestors of the Hungarians known as Csángós (wanderers?) settled in Moldavia. Although the Hungarian conquerors initially occupied the Viennese basin as well, they rapidly withdrew from there to the line of the Lajta river. In the end, the Moldavian Csángó were the only remaining block of Hungarian extraction beyond the Carpathian basin.

The Tearful Chronicle

$\mathscr{I}$n 1221 the latest crusade was under way or actually slowly dragging along in the Holy Land, fought by unenthusiastic forces whose religious convictions and beliefs in the purpose of the crusade were equally doubtful. Suddenly electrifying news spread throughout Europe, particularly through the monasteries. An old legend had again come to life about a group of Christians who in ancient times became isolated in the East and there flourished. This was the legend of the Land of Prester John. According to the news, armies from this land had attacked the eastern provinces of the Saracens and were on their way to liberate the Holy Land. Actually, there never was a Land of Prester John. Who then were those who really did begin a march from Central Asia, although not toward Jerusalem but – as their final goal – against Rome?

At the same time, or somewhat earlier, a belief or legend arose in Hungary, where even though the administration was in firm control, there was a feeling of impending doom, and where indeed there were many minor dangers to be dealt with. Certain rumors spread about some alarming preparations being made along the major highway of migration along which our ancestors had traveled to arrive in their new homeland. It is possible that this unexpected and unwelcome information came to the Hungarians in the Carpathian basin as a result of some tentative attempts to search for their original home. It is certain that several successive attempts had been made to find some Hungarian groups who had separated from the main body at the time of migration and who had remained in the east. When finally a successful contact was made with Hungarians in far away Baskiria, it was too late. By the time they were discovered, they were being swept away by a destructive flood of farther eastern forces who suddenly and justifiably spread terror throughout Europe. It is typical that while the naive European Christians were still expecting succor from the eastern Christians of Prester John's land, the much better informed conquerors were fully aware of the misinformation that preceded them. They overran the still Christian Gruz with the advanced troops carrying crosses to mislead the unsuspecting inhabitants.

We will omit a number of other details, since here we must discuss the events as they relate to Transylvania. Suffice it to say that at long last the steppe-dwelling Mongolian tribes joined together – a traditional arrangement of the nomadic empires – and advanced from the heart of Asia toward the heart of Europe. The unified assault, traditionally referred to in Hungary as the Tatar Invasion, reached the Carpathian basin in the spring of 1241. By this time the mists surrounding the land of Prester John have long since dissipated. The Dominican friar Julianus and his brethren, who went in search of the Baskirian Hungarians, alerted the religious and lay leaders of Europe to the impending danger. The Hungarian King Béla IV (1234-1270) was in receipt of a letter, written in Tatar but clearly understandable following successive translations: "I, the Khan, emissary of the Heavenly King, who was granted the power on earth to raise my vassals and oppress my opponents, am amazed at you, king of Hungary. I have sent you thirty emissaries already. Why don't you send even one of them back to me with a letter containing your reply? I know you are a rich and powerful king. You have many soldiers and you rule your large country by yourself. Thus, it may be difficult for you to submit to me, but it would be better and more salutary for you if you would submit to me. I have also learned that you are keeping my Cumanian servants under your protection. I am therefore instructing you to stop protecting them and avoid confronting me on their behalf. They could escape easily, having no houses and could flee, wandering with their tents, but you who live in a house and have castles and cities will not be able to escape from my hands."

This letter is a marvel of the Asiatic style. It is convincing, and not exactly friendly. Yet, as it became obvious soon, it was prophetic. There had to be a king on the throne who had confidence in himself. If he gave in, he was no longer a king but a vassal. Concerning the eastern Cumanians mentioned in the letter, their accommodation ultimately turned out to be detrimental, but not for the reasons given in the Khan's letter. The appearance of the still nomadic, pagan, Cumanians in the Great Plain upset the internal peace of the country and raised discontent and anger with the king's decision at the precise moment when there was the greatest need for harmony. These Cumanians, whose customs and morals were similar to those of the original Hungarian conquerors, could hardly fit in with the now well settled Hungarians, even in peacetime. They were thoroughly familiar with the tactics and mentality of the approaching Tatars – we may as well begin to call them by that name – about whom the Hungarians knew very little. These Cumanians would be badly needed, but they were again, misunderstood. The Hungarians, opposing the king's wishes, considered the Cumanians to be advance accomplices of the Tatars, killed their tribal chieftain and expelled them. This left them even more defenseless.

In March 1241, the forces of Batu Khan crossed the Carpathians simultaneously through the northern, eastern and southern passes. Their *Blitzkrieg*, which caused Béla IV and his family to flee first to the castle of Knin in Dalmacia, then to Trorig and finally to the island of Ciovo, ground to a halt in Hungary. This was due not so much to the Hungarian resistance, but rather to internal problems caused by the death of the Mongolian Great Khan. Their elan, their methods of warfare and their customary, long continued absences from home, do not seem to suggest that they had reached the possible limits of their conquest in the Carpathian basin.

Their main force moved south, along the right bank of the Danube, in the spring of 1242. In the Balkans, almost in passing, they subjugated the Bulgarians. A large sub-group ravaged Transylvania again, and departed through the eastern passes of the Carpathians. Behind them the country was devastated, just how badly is a matter of ancient debate. The contemporary descriptions are apocalyptic. The "Tearful" Chronicle of the Italian Master Rogerius, canon of Várad and later archbishop of Spalato, details it for posterity. His detailed and impassioned description sounds very much like an eyewitness account and radiates the heat of things seen and suffered. His words evoke a documentary moving picture and show us houses totally destroyed by fire, despoiled churches, and the bloody, decaying cadavers of raped and murdered inhabitants. Those who hid in the deep forests and in the swamps were lured out with ruses and false promises, and were then massacred in turn.

The modern reader discovers only gradually that the eminent Rogerius is internally contradictory. Principally, if his description had been accurate and factual, Béla IV would have been unable to rebuild quite so quickly after his return following the withdrawal of the Tatars. Many of his programs, particularly the extensive and accelerated erection of towns and castles, postulates the presence of a very large work force, huge numbers of artisans and even more helpers and, in addition, adequate building supplies and, most importantly, food for these multitudes.

Regardless how questionable the direct and indirect damages of the Tatar invasion may have been, it seems likely that the damages in Transylvania were greater than elsewhere. The harm must have been greatest in the valleys and among the population of the great basins. The mountain dwellers and their herds and settlements were probably only minimally affected, or not at all. Neither the Tatars nor the epidemics that followed their invasion penetrated the mountainous regions. Neither then, nor later. This again changed the ethnic ratios. We mentioned the significant Hungarian-Saxon-Székely emigration to beyond the Carpathians, primarily to the Havasalföld, but also to Moldavia. After the disaster, Transylvania exerted a strong attraction. This was promoted by administrative reorganizations which linked certain Transcarpathian units with units on this side of the Carpathians. Within these linked units, changes in ownership and domicile could be easily undertaken. The administration "straddling" the Carpathians became a bridge for egress and ingress, first for the former and then for the latter.

The administration was undergoing almost continuous changes. Throughout the country the former royal county organizations were falling apart. Béla IV, sharing the regal burden of reconstruction with the magnates and with the cities, looses some of his power. There is a "Quid pro quo". Whoever gets permission to build a fortress for the protection of the country may mobilize forces against internal enemies as well.

At this time, Transylvania's regional independence became stronger rather than weaker and the personality and responsibilities of the Transylvanian voivode was undergoing frequent changes. The Székely and Saxon *szék* autonomy was maintained, but then a number of voivodes and *ispán*s were charged with the establishment and supervision of new, smaller areas. A number of these now had a Romanian majority.

It was a strange and colorful world. Just as in other parts of the Hungarian kingdom, namely in the crown lands, ethnic origin was now less significant. It was the language and the religious affiliations that become the dominant factors and not the "political" considerations. Even more important than the old tribal-national organization was the individual's place in the stratification of the classes and the accompanying division of labor. This, of course, pertained only to those members of the communities who had been fully accepted and assimilated into them.

Even though undefeated, the Tartars were gone, but the threat remained. No year went by without the news of an impending invasion. Even though these invasions may not have taken place, or may not reached the Carpathian basin, they were not without foundation. It was for this reason that Béla IV received the fleeing son of the Russian Great Prince from Tsernygov, Rostislav, and accepted him as his son-in-law. He later assisted him with an army in the latter's Halics campaign. It seems that the king of Hungary did have an effective army, which also argues against the alleged total destruction of the country. Béla IV also took back the formerly expelled Cumanians, but this time they were given an area in the central region of the Great Plain for settlement and grazing.

There came now another experiment with the crusaders – and this brings us back to Transylvania.

We cannot compete with the terse statement in the *Historical Chronology of Hungary* and quote the following passage from it. (Note the two italicized passages: a feudal contract mentions Romanians in two places): "On June 2, 1247, Béla IV contracts with the Hospitaler [St. John's or Crusader] Order. Among other things, the king gives the Crusaders the Szörénység, except for the land of the *Romanian voivodate*, all the way to the Olt river, Cumania beyond the Olt and the southeastern corner of Transylvania, with its revenues and judicial powers and permits them to participate in the transport and export of salt. He also supports them in the erection of fortresses in Cumania. The Crusaders make a commitment to improve their feudal lands, increase its population, and protect their territory together with the *Romanians [Olati]*. In addition, they will render military assistance in case of a Hungarian campaign into Bulgaria, Greece or Cumania."

The Hospitalers relinquish their feudal lands sometimes between 1258 and 1260, thus, they did not have to be expelled. The problem was not that they had been building fortresses, but rather that they had not done so. They leave. Hungary and, particularly, Transylvania had very poor luck with these not very knightly Crusader knights. *Nota bene:* Salt! When Béla IV, in May 1242, immediately after the withdrawal of the Tatars, appointed a certain Paul of the Gerenye family as "Commissioner of Reconstruction" of the territories to the west of the Danube, the principal task with which he was charged was the suppression of highway robbery, the collection of the scattered population – and the reopening of the Transylvanian salt mines.

In 1257, Béla IV appointed his oldest son, the crown prince, as Prince of Transylvania. Stephen was approximately eighteen-years-old at this time. His wife, whose Christian name was Elizabeth, was the daughter of one of the Cumanian chieftains in Hungary. Stephen, who very shortly promoted himself from prince to junior king, at times contracted with his father about his lands and rights and at times attacked him. He was no longer just the Prince of Transylvania. His domains included everything east of the Danube. His younger brother, Prince Béla, won Slavonia for himself. Thus, the king held only Transdanubia and a small area in the north for himself. The issue obviously was not Transylvania alone, but the burning ambition of the crown prince that the king was unable to satisfy. Yet, the relationship between them became a contributing factor in deciding that the fate of Transylvania and that of the country as a whole did not follow the same path.

As far as the Tatars were concerned, there was a gap that spanned two generations. They appeared inside of the Carpathians again in 1285. Ranging through the Verecke pass, they advanced as far as the city of Pest. This was not a concentrated attack against Europe, but only a large scale, exploratory robber campaign. When barely a month later, they retired toward the east, through Transylvania, there Loránd of the Borsa family, the Transylvanian voivode defeated them in battle and took many prisoners. This led to serious future difficulties.

In the meantime, from having been prince of Transylvania and junior king, Stephen V became king, but only for two years (1270-1272). He was succeeded on the throne by Ladislas IV (the Cumanian), the son of the "Cumanian woman". The epithet, Cumanian, was not without foundation. Even though Ladislas IV's wife was an Anjou princess, the daughter of the Neapolitan-Sicilian king, Charles I, the king was partial to his maternal relatives and to the relatives of his Cumanian mistress. Furthermore, he enlisted the Transylvanian captive Tatars into his army and used them in internal warfare. He later had to take a solemn oath before the Archbishop of Esztergom that he would not grant offices to those who had not been baptized. He abandoned the Tatars just as he abandoned his mistress, and he took back his wife, the Anjou Elizabeth. (To what extent? The chronicles are silent about any offspring.) But this again is not part of the history of Transylvania.

Just as in the west, there was a tendency in Transylvania to replace the royal domains and the revenue generated by service in these domains, with domains and revenues – principally in specie – held by the magnates. The royal counties were slowly being replaced by counties of the nobility. This represented a direct challenge to all the previous privileges and autonomies granted by the king, and became a source of much internal strife. Old interests were smashed by the new ones. In the meantime, the increasingly numerous and important Romanian population, this side of the Carpathians, did not yet have or expect the advantages granted to the Székely and Saxon populations. The weakening of the central administration and the departure of the Hospitalers made secession very appealing to the Transcarpathian Romanians. Such an attempt resulted in the death of the Romanian voivode Litvoj, the lord of the Szörény, killed during a Hungarian punitive campaign. A few years later, the Szörény Banate, which represented a Transylvanian and Hungarian clenched fist aimed at the heart of the Balkans, was lost to the Hungarian Crown, and so was Cumania. This is just the beginning of the times when new "autonomies" rise alongside the old ones and occasionally in opposition to them. The already strongly muscular or still growing magnate families created feudal fiefdoms, questioned the royal authority and, in effect, ruled small separate "kingdoms", to the detriment of the whole country.

At this time, in Transylvania, these petty rulers were not yet native sons and represented "foreign" dignitaries. The most eminent among them is the voivode Ladislas Khan, who became well known when he got the Crown of St. Stephen into his hands and refused to give it up to its rightful owner, the Anjou Charles Robert. It was only after decades of bitter domestic fighting that the legitimate ruler could regain control over Transylvania from Ladislas Khan and from his sons. Even then the success was incomplete. There was hardly any voivode or other royal official who did not attempt to create an autonomous fiefdom for himself at the cost of the royal authority. There were some which were evanescent, while others were preserved for a life-time and were even bequeathed to sons and grandsons. The Transylvanian Saxons were not exactly angels either. During their ongoing fight with the bishop of Gyulafehérvár, the king was finally forced to call in the Great Plain Cumanians to teach them a lesson.

The chapter by Master Rogerius which dealt with the Tatar invasion and was consequently entitled *The Tearful Chronicle*, could be continued at this time. The western parts of the country were freed from any further Mongolian threats after the "lesser Tatar invasion" of 1285. Transylvania was still subject periodically to the "Eastern plague". In the foreground of the Carpathians, the Tatar presence underwent changes but was persistent. This restless band of brigands, always ready for raids or for campaigns to stock the ever flourishing slave markets of the Crimea with live human merchandise, was more recently less likely to act on their own, but offered its mercenary services to other leaders. It made very little difference to the subjects of their attention.

The ethnic structure of Transylvania was modified by the immigrants who fled to the more protected Carpathian basin from the regions outside the Carpathians which were still subject to Tatar harassment. There was a particularly heavy influx from among the Romanian mountain shepherd tribes who had made the trip across the Carpathians between Transylvania and the Havasalföld, and between Transylvania and Moldavia, twice each year for many years. They were further motivated by the fact that being Greek Orthodox, they were exempt from the church tax (tithe) and had to pay only the "one fiftieth" tax for their herds. Their settlements were well

defined in increasing numbers, by the partly wood-
en and partly masonry churches and monasteries.

Finally, a tearful chronicle, no less lamentable
than the one written by Master Rogerius, could be
written about the fires and ashes of the peasant
revolt led by Antal Budai Nagy (1437). The feudalism that eventually reached Transylvanian society
was even more unstructured than its original
Hungarian model. In Transylvania it never developed fully along the classic lines of the West. The
changes in the interrelation of the classes, the
increasing arrogance of the nobility and the continu-
ing threats from the Balkans which imposed increasing financial burdens on them, led to rebellion and it
was by no means the lowest levels of society,
Hungarian or Romanian, which revolted. The
Transylvanian rebels proudly called themselves "the
association of the Hungarian and Romanian inhabitants of Transylvania", and "free men". These com-
ments, typically directed against the nobility,
announced the Hussite program for social equality.
They also clearly followed a Hussite example
when they entrenched themselves, as though on a
"Transylvanian Mount Tabor", on the extensive
plateau of Mount Bábolna, near the community of
Alparét, in the county of Doboka. (László Makkai.)
Just like in the later Dózsa rebellion, the leader of
this rebellion, Antal Budai Nagy, is not a serf but a
gentry. In these rebellions the organizers and leaders were not those who had suffered the most, but
mainly those who had something to loose beside
their life. Even a significant percentage of the large
group of followers came from the lower but proper-

tied classes and not from among the "have nots".
They represented a group who were deprived of
something they had acquired. After several victories
and conditional agreements, this bloody revolt came
to an end. The major factor in its collapse was that
the demands of the participating gentry were met,
while the other participating groups were ignored.
Thus, the unity of the rebellion fell apart.

This movement was not triggered by an ad hoc
displeasure, a sudden rage or an overwhelming pas-
sion. It represented the long-term goals of its leaders. This is shown by the fact that they had met
annually on Mount Bábolna to discuss their situation
and actual demands. This dangerous situation was
responsible for the emergence, on the other side, of
the "three Transylvanian nations", an association of
the Hungarian nobility, the Székelys and the Saxons,
which then remained for a very long time an important factor and a much cited base in the constitutional struggles in Transylvania's future history. The
triple union was first ratified by the delegates of the
three parties in Kápolna in September 1437, and was
renewed in February 1438 in Torda, the site of
numerous future Transylvanian Diets. The rebellion
led by Antal Budai Nagy and characterized by
extreme cruelty on both sides, sapped Transylvania's
inner strength and cohesion, just when a new and
enormous danger arose – from the east.

Raven on High

*I*n 1326 Brussa (the present Burma) became the capital of the Ottoman Turks. It was still in Asia Minor, but at its western edge. In 1362 the capital was already in Drinapoli (the present Edirne), well this side of the Sea of Marmara and in the Balkans. The ring tightened around the unfortunate capital of the Eastern Roman Empire, but Byzantium did not fall until 1453 at which time it became Istambul, or in its shorter form, Stambul. During these years, the sabers of the rapacious Turkish Sultanate reached ever further across the Balkans, toward the more precious parts of Europe, to conquer them, or at the very least to hurt them. By sea the primary target was Venice, as the principal guardian of the east-west trade routes. On land the main thrust was in the direction of Stambul-Sofia-Belgrade-Budapest-Vienna. This route was impossible unless the armies could cross the soft underbelly of Transylvania, the Hungarian Délvidék.

When Béla IV received the Tatar letter quoted above, presumably in 1240, Pope Gregory IX still urged him to lead a crusade for the liberation of the Holy Land. By this time the trend there had been reversed. In 1244, Jerusalem was lost and in 1291 the last Palestinian fortress of the crusaders, Acre, was captured by the Moslems, that is by the Mameluk Sultanate of Egypt.

This was the last chapter in the series of offensive "Holy Wars" for the recovery of the cradle of Christianity from the pagans, and for the control of the eastern commerce. At this point, the penetration of the pagans into southeastern Europe and the Balkans should have been prevented by a new crusade. The bastion of the eastern Apostolic Cross had fallen, and the western bastion must now be defended.

In Hungary, in the meantime the nearly 40 year rule of Charles Robert, of the House of Anjou, came to an end and the 40 year rule of his son Louis I (the Great) (1342-1382) began. He also became King of Poland in 1370, and spent enormous energy and huge sums of money on the conquest (re-conquest) of the throne of Naples for the House of Anjou. His rule, also not free from internal dissensions, was followed by the half century rule of Sigismund of Luxembourg (1387-1437). Sigismund first ruled as the consort of Louis's daughter Maria (1382-1395) and, after her early death in an accident, he held the throne alone. In Sigismund's day, the Turkish conquest had progressed to the point where the Balkan buffer states were gone, and the Sultan's armies attacked the Hungarian homeland directly.

Sigismund fought two battles with the Turks. At Nicapolis, in 1396, the European crusader knights, led by him, were defeated, and in 1428 the campaign to recover Galambóc, an important bastion defending Belgrade, lost the previous year, ended in disaster. These were ominous signs.

Between these two lost battles, in 1407, but we don't know where, a child was born, who was the first one to recognize the real significance of this new eastern threat. The origins of János Hunyadi are unclear. He was thought to be Romanian (his father was a *boyar* who moved from Havaselve), and he was also thought to be the illegitimate son of King Sigismund. This is not our concern. His deeds speak for themselves. All we know is that he started from a relatively low rank, served in numerous campaigns and became the leading military commander of 15th century Europe. It cannot be denied that he gained the respect of his rulers. At the end of his life he owned a property of 2 million hectares, one quarter of which was in Transylvania. It is here that he built, almost in the face of the Turks, his mighty and justly celebrated fortress of Vajdahunyad. This was where his two sons, László and Matthias grew up.

János Hunyadi thought and acted more as a vassal than as an independent landowner and devoted almost all of his enormous revenues to the war against the Turks. We may ignore most of his heroic battles, both those he won and those he lost, and concentrate on the one for which the bells still toll.

In 1456, three years after having captured Byzantium-Constantinople and converting it into Stambul, Sultan Mohammed II took the field in person, and departed for the siege of Nándorfehérvár. This city is today known as Belgrade and is the capital of Serbia. In those days, it was a fortress not far from the Hungarian border and a key point along the military highway leading to Buda and Vienna.

The relieving forces under Hunyadi were composed of three elements. Alongside the Hungarian
nobility and the paid mercenaries, he used the lin-
gering emotional appeal of the crusades and called
the lower classes to arms. This was a very coura-
geous act, since these were the people who in the
past, oppressed and exploited, rose against their
masters on more than one occasion. Under
Nándorfehérvár they became comrades in arms. In
recruiting the crusaders and also during the battle,
Hunyadi's strong right arm was a Franciscan friar,
John Capistran, the future Saint John Capistran, a
rigidly moral, fiery priest and a merciless inquisitor.

The Christians won a resounding victory. The
wounded Sultan was carried from the field by his
guards, more dead than alive. This victory of
Nándorfehérvár halted the Ottoman expansion into
Europe for more than a century. It was a huge
opportunity waiting to be exploited, but only the
bells tolled.

Today, few are aware of it, even in Hungary, but
wherever in the world day after day the bells are
rung in the churches at noon, this is done in memory
of the victory János Hunyadi gained on July 22, 1456
under the walls of Nándorfehérvár. According to
one version, it was Pope Callixtus III, who in his
happiness over this victory ordered all the bells in
Rome to ring at noon. In fact, the order to ring the
bells preceded the battle and was issued on June 29.
The Pope wished to use the bells to plead with the
heavens so that the battle which may have meant
the survival of Christianity be decided in their favor.
Yet the earlier version is not entirely incorrect. The

fact that the noon ringing was perpetuated, was indeed in celebration of the victory. (Later, when the memory of Nándorfehérvár paled, the custom was maintained since it announced the middle of the day in all the Catholic lands and called the faithful to the table.)

Only a few weeks after the battle, another bell tolled for János Hunyadi, the funeral bell. The plague swept through the camp and he became one of the victims. That same fall John Capistran also died. The loss of these two champions of victory at a time when the country was again in a leadership crisis and slipping into anarchy, could have been fatal to the defense against the Turks. Hunyadi's career started in Transylvania, raced like a comet across the skies and ended in his premature death. Fortunately, there was another Hunyadi to carry on.

In the interregnum between the mid-century struggles for the throne, János Hunyadi carried the title of regent and was in fact practically the king. He was a late-medieval, self made man who carved his path with his sword. When his brilliant career came to an end in 1452, his oldest son, the 23-year-old László, represented an almost dynastic successor. Several planned marriages would have connected him to either competing or associated magnate families but no marriage was ever solemnized. He piled honor upon honor. In 1452 he was already *ispán* of Pozsony, one year later he was prince of Croatia-Slovenia. At the death of his father, he was *ispán* of Temes, and now he inherited his father's estates and most of his titles.

The king of Hungary at this time was the posthumous son of the first Habsburg ruler, Albert (1437-1439), Ladislas V (1440-1457) who was crowned as an infant, being born some months after his father's death. There was at the same time another king of Hungary, Wladislas I (1440-1444), from the House of Jagello. In 1444 he accompanied Hunyadi on a well-intentioned but foolhardy crusade against the Turks. After a few minor victories, he was soundly defeated at Várna. The king was left dead on the battle field. Nobody knows where he was buried. Thus, the Habsburg child-king, Ladislas V, was left alone and for a few years Hunyadi acted as regent. Let us return, however, to our historical sequence.

The struggle between the Hungarian magnates became accentuated after the death of the head of the Hunyadi family and they all competed in trying to diminish the patrimony and titles of his son László. The challenge became increasingly overt. When Ladislas V and the Hunyadi's main antagonist, Ulrik Cillei, during their travels in Transylvania and southern Hungary expressed a desire to possess Vajdahunyad, László Hunyadi and his adherents murdered Cillei. The king was terrified and granted amnesty under oath. A few months later, he had László taken prisoner in Buda and had him beheaded.

The scene was a horrible one. During the public execution, organized with the participation of the Court, the executioner struck three times, but the young man was still alive. According to the customs of the times, he should now have been pardoned. Ladislas V, only 17-years-old but a neurotic and pre-

maturely roue lout, nodded and the executioner
struck for the fourth time. This time the head was
separated from the trunk. The king again took fright
and fled, first to Vienna and then to Prague. He
could easily do this, since he was simultaneously
Duke of Austria and King of Bohemia. He dragged
the younger son, Matthias, with him as a hostage. We
can see the hand of fate when this very fall Ladislas
succumbs to the plague. Parenthetically – still in
1438, a marauding Turkish band, augmented by
Romanian and Serb auxiliaries, invades Transylvania
through the southern Transylvanian county of Hunyad.
They were being guided through the Carpathian
passes by a certain voivode of Havaselve, Dracul
Vlad. It was on his guarantee as a former officer of
Sigismund that Szászsebes surrendered – to its
destruction. They then succeeded to capture Gyulafehérvár and a number of other smaller towns or
their outlying settlements, although they failed to
take Szeben. They withdrew after a long and cruel
rapine, loaded with treasure and captives.

If we now wish to investigate the model for the
currently universally familiar monster: Dracula, who
is so intimately associated with Transylvania then,
according to one version, we do not have to look
further than the above Vlad. Earlier and by the grace
of the king, he had been invested with the
Hungarian Dragon Knighthood. It was precisely this
knightly designation (Dragon-Dracul-Devil) which
induced his own Romanians to attach the name
Dracula to him and make him the seminal figure in a
recurrent cycle of legends which came to yet another flowering in the 19th and 20th centuries.

According to another tradition, this seminal figure was younger and dates to the age of Matthias; what's more, he was also a voivode of Havaselve. He became notorious primarily by his predilection for having his enemies and challengers impaled as a form of execution. He was not an invader and, in fact, when the Turks took control of the Havaselve, he fled to Hungary.

One thing is certain. Dracula, this monster, was a native of this region. He existed, was notorious for his cruelties – sadly not a rarity in these times – and his fame spread from this location. The first ones to spread the stories about this dreadful ogre were the loquacious humanists – one could call them rumor-mongers – of the court of Matthias.

The lout Ladislas V took the child Matthias Hunyadi with him as a captive. He did not, however, raise a hand against him. Generally, those few brief moments when the executioner took four strokes to severe László Hunyadi's neck caused considerable consternation even in the bloodthirsty era which gave rise to the Dracula legend.

It was the psychological after-effect of this botched execution that the Hunyadi family again gained precedence, could no longer be ignored and carried the favor of the bulk of the politically important mid-nobility with it. He who creates a martyr, multiplies the number of his own enemies.

There was also a peculiar "Hunyadi tradition". The tradition was more than an inheritance, more than all the offices and more than the enormous patrimony which was so envied by the Cilleis, that it led to a break with László and to the death of Ulrik

Cillei. We have emphasized already that János Hunyadi treated his lands like a feudal property, and
used them on behalf of the king and for the protection of the country. He was also strongly in favor of
giving an ear not only to the central authority and to
the oligarchy which continuously attempted to chis-
el away at this central authority, but also to the
nobility in the counties and the rural districts, and
even to the urban bourgeoisie which, compared to
the rest of Europe, was relatively poorly developed
in Hungary. He did this primarily to "spread" the
necessary burden of the military-defensive costs to
the widest possible base. Yet, the popularity and
goodwill so gained among the middle classes also
became a part of the Hunyadi inheritance. These
classes will suffer a major disappointment very
shortly, particularly in Transylvania.

At the end of 1457, a few weeks after the death of
Ladislas V from the plague, Matthias Hunyadi was
set free from his captivity in Prague. (The price of
his freedom was his engagement to the Bohemian
princess Catherine Podjebrad, the daughter of his
jailer, which ordinarily may be a good omen in case
of a serious love affair, but which, in this instance,
was a pawn to a not very successful marriage.)
Shortly thereafter, on January 23 and 24, 1458
Matthias was elected king (1458-1490). After the dis-
appearance of the House of Árpád, the country once
again had a native king, assuring the nation of its
right to self-determination and of its freedom of
choice.

There are two dates because Matthias was proclaimed king both at the traditional assembly site of

Hungary, the Rákos mező, but also in Buda, on the ice of the frozen Danube, by 15,000 noblemen assembled for the purpose by his uncle, Mihály Szilágyi, the eminent magnate. The acclamation was unanimous.

Mihály Szilágyi acted as guardian and regent. He began his regency and made decisions concerning taxes, goods and authorities, far removed from the spirit of János Hunyadi. In this, later he was followed by Matthias himself. The central authority had to be strengthened. Since the great ones being great remained great, all these regulations were made at the expense of the smaller people, the middle-nobility, the Saxons and the Székelys. There were movements and rebellions in Transylvania "against Buda", which gave rise to reprisals and even to a punitive campaign.

This region had a bad start with the new king, who was born in Kolozsvár and grew up in Vajdahunyad. Later, having replaced his uncle for acting arbitrarily in his name, (he sent Szilágyi to fight against the Turk where he was killed), he strengthened the defenses of Transylvania against attack from the south. The Saxon cities were building fortifications and even in the villages the churches were fortified. The endeavors of the king and of the population were mutually supportive, and not only among the Saxons, but among the Hungarians and Székelys as well.

Matthias decided to use Visegrád, rather than the distant and exposed Vajdahunyad, as the beneficiary of his generosity, and endowed it above all others with splendid adornments. He moved his mother to Buda. Vajdahunyad was not forgotten, however, and also received Renaissance treasures and structural improvements. The magnates of Transylvania did likewise, in competition, with their own castles.

It was characteristic of Matthias's policies that while he was convinced that the country had to be strengthened to be able to resist the Turks, he withdrew his attention from the Balkans and turned his eyes toward Vienna and Prague. He wished to control all effective forces against the Turks from there. This attempt, while well intentioned and not unreasonable, accomplished very little. The Transylvanian inheritance from his father was very helpful to Matthias in the beginning. Even in the organization of the famous Black Army one can recognize János Hunyadi's influence, who always favored mercenary forces. In the final analysis, however, this otherwise exceptionally gifted son did not benefit much from this spiritual inheritance.

It must be mentioned about Transylvania in the age of the Hunyadis that at this time the Romanian elite – whether assimilated or not – could enter the ranks of the Hungarian nobility. Saxon independence was frequently manifested by their limiting the settlement of non-Germans in their cities. Székely freedom was endangered not only by external forces but also from internal dissensions, "societal pincers", in which class interests outweighed the interests of the entire all-Székely community. Even though the extra-Carpathian regions increasingly slipped out from under Hungarian control, the export and import of goods to and from this area was controlled by Transylvania and was very profitable.

The principal Hungarian exports were precious metals and live animals. The main imported items were textiles, particularly woolens. The principal Transylvanian export items were mining products. The bulk of the Hungarian cattle export came from the Great Plain. Moldavia and the Havasalföld were the major markets and transfer points for the textile products coming through Hungary from the west. Since a number of cities had the right to collect duties, this was very lucrative for Transylvania.

The late Roman, Gothic and late Gothic remains indicate that the majority of the late medieval architectural and artistic efforts were directed toward the churches. It is much less evident, and shows up later in the castles, mansions and, finally, in the houses of the bourgeoisie. Matthias himself was born in one of the Gothic homes in Kolozsvár. We know of several artists of the Transylvanian Gothic, such as the painter Miklós Kolozsvári, who presumably ran a large atelier and his two sons, Márton and György, who were both sculptors of genius. We must again emphasize that the Transylvanian Gothic represents a sharp dividing line between the two distinct areas of Europe.

Creative arts may be enjoyed everywhere in the world, but in the culture of Transylvania the major emphasis must be placed on the emergence of the mother tongue. Why Hungarian became so strong, relative to Latin, at this time is not at all clear. In Buda and Visegrád, among the humanists in the court of Matthias, Latin was not only the language of the church or of the administration, but enjoyed almost complete dominance even in interpersonal communication. This was universal, since Latin is the Esperanto of the age.

By contrast, in Transylvania the Saxons, while preventing the settlement of non-Germans, maintained their own language and literature, even though their leaders were all fluent in Latin. Partly under Hussite influences and also, of course, in monastic circles, numerous parts of the Scriptures were translated into Hungarian in Transylvania. And this was not all. Romanian literacy was more advanced in the Carpathian basin than beyond it, even though there the preponderance of Romanians was much greater.

We must rely on estimates alone, but at the death of Matthias, at the end of the 15th century, Transylvania had approximately slightly less than 500,000 inhabitants. About 60 percent were Hungarian, including of course the Székelys, 24 percent were already Romanian, and the Saxons made up the remaining 16 percent.

The Remainder

$\mathscr{L}$et it begin with a family name, or rather with several names of the same family. The progenitor of the Szapolyai or Zápolya was a certain László, who under the name of Vajdafi, left the service of János Hunyadi and became, among other things, *ispán* of the salt monopoly. One of his two sons, Imre, added to the family fortunes by making large loans to King Matthias for very large returns. His younger brother, István, acquired undying fame – and titles and estates, by convincing the nobles, vacillating after Matthias's death, to elect the otherwise eligible Wladislas II (1490-1516). Imre did not consider himself to be eligible, but since the election of a Hungarian king could become a reality, he did raise his son as a person eligible for the kingship. He did much to accomplish this, even though he did not do much else. All these matters were more or less related to Transylvania.

After Matthias's death and the end of the Hunyadi era, the two most important dates are 1514 and 1526, the dates of two related tragedies. But first there was 1506. Wladislas II, to celebrate the birth of the crown prince, wished to collect an old tax from the Székelys, which they refused with the justification that as nobles, they were no longer subject to taxation. The Székely rebellion was defeated, with Szeben Saxon participation, under the leadership of Pál Tomori, who at this time was "just" a soldier, but later became archbishop of Kalocsa and perished at the battle of Mohács. When the Székelys sent a detachment to take revenge on the Saxons, it was led by a György Dózsa de Makfalva. He may be, but probably is not, the peasant leader György Dózsa.

The campaign of 1514 started out as a crusade. The army, which could be joined by the "ordinary people", should have marched against the Turks. The nationwide, serious dissatisfaction – not so much of the poorest strata, but of the landed serfs who participated in the production of goods and had thus something to loose – turned the crusaders against the nobility. It appeared almost as the first breath of the Reformation. At the head of this destructive movement, later known as the Dózsa Peasant Revolt, marched and fought a number of Franciscan friars. Some of them – who survived long enough – were among the first Protestant preachers.

Although the movement was led militarily by György Dózsa, who was clearly considered a Transylvanian, it concentrated primarily on the Great Plains. In Transylvania, it did not touch the Székely regions, and touched only a few of the Hungarian areas. These included some important, and justly unhappy, salt and mining cities such as Dés, Torda, Abrudbánya, Zalatna and Torockó.

At this time, since 1510, the twenty-year-old Szapolyai (Zápolya), the future king, was voivode of Transylvania. His first military triumph was the destruction of the Dózsa army approaching from the

Great Plain. The battle of Temesvár put an end to the largest peasant revolt in Hungarian history. Three years later, in 1517, he was again the executioner of another, smaller revolt, this time in Transylvania. At this time the enterprising voivode confiscated the property of the participants for the Crown. This was contrary to Székely tradition. It had always been one of the privileges of the Székelys that in case of disloyalty, the property of the guilty person went to his relatives. There was no collective punishment for individual crime.

Between the time of these two campaigns of Szapolyai, Wladislas II died and was succeeded by his ten-year-old son, Louis II (1516-1526). It was decreed that the voivode of Transylvania was responsible for the defense of Transylvania alone, while the governor of Temes was responsible for the Temesköz. In return, they had to fight in any other part of the country only if the entire country was in deadly peril. This decree formally codified a regionalization which had been a practical reality for some time. King Louis II was already married. At the age of 10, in 1515, he married the nine-year-old Maria Habsburg, the daughter of Philip le Bel and Johanna the Insane. At the same time, his brother-in-law, Ferdinand Habsburg, married Louis's sister, Anna Jagello. Thus, a two-fold marriage united the Czech-Hungarian House of Jagello with the Austrian House of Habsburg. This was to have enormous consequences in the near future.

In 1520, when the Jagello boy and the Habsburg girl may have already consummated their marriage in Buda, Suleiman II, known to history as the Great, and as the Conqueror, assumed the throne in Stambul, which he would hold for 46 years. This took place on September 22, which was too late in the year for a Turkish style campaign. In June 1521, however, the Turkish armies appeared before Nándorfehérvár, followed very soon by the Padishah. After a siege of a month and a half, the city was taken and the armies returned to Stambul, so that Suleiman the Great could celebrate the first anniversary of his rule at home. This, both symbolically and in reality, brought to an end the breathing space that János Hunyadi gained in 1436, when he was triumphant at this very same place. Now the Ottoman advance seemed irresistible.

A series of frontier bastions were conquered. The Hungarian line of defense was gradually pushed back toward the northwest. This continued until 1526, when Suleiman, advancing along his usual route slowly and almost leisurely, crossed the Száva on a newly built bridge and approached Mohács with an enormous army. The king hesitated. Should he again mobilize the lower orders? On the news of the Turkish preparations, he mobilized only 20 percent of the serfs in March, and only 50 percent in July. Finally, at the beginning of August, on his way toward Mohács, he ordered the mobilization of all forces. He also sent János Szapolyai, voivode of Transylvania, contradictory instructions. First, he asked him to bring his army to the probable field of battle, then he told him to stay away. In spite of this, the rumors were rife afterward, accusing the voivode of having started out toward Mohács, but then intentionally delaying his arrival on the plains of battle.

His army of ten thousand men remained untouched, while the king's and Tomori's army of 25,000 – *nota bene,* mostly foreign mercenaries – was essentially annihilated on August 29, 1526 on the field of Mohács. Both the prelate-commander-in-chief and the king perished. The latter drowned in the flooded river Csele, although there was a widespread belief that he was killed by his own men.

Szapolyai remained at Szeged, Queen Maria took a boat up the Danube and the armies of Suleiman – burning and looting – sauntered into the unprotected Buda. North of Buda, at Pilismarót, the refugees formed a camp, but the country lost more people here from illness and hunger than it did at Mohács. Since this campaign was more in the nature of a final warning for Vienna, the Turks evacuated Hungary, leaving only a line of defended fortresses in the Szerémség. Thus, the terrible defeat did not affect Transylvania directly. Indirectly, however, the effects were momentous. Szapolyai, who probably stayed away from Mohács intentionally, was acclaimed king on two separate occasions in the newly "liberated" country, once in October at Tokaj and again in November in Székesfehérvár. In the latter place he actually had the crown placed on his head in the presence of the nobles assembled there. He immediately appointed the enormously wealthy Péter Perényi voivode of Transylvania, who then betrayed him within the year. John (Szapolyai) I (1526-1540) did not stay king alone for very long. In December, in Pozsony, the nobles assembled there acclaimed Ferdinand I (1526-1546), the Habsburg brother-in-law of the late Louis II, King of Hungary. Ferdinand was already King of Bohemia and will shortly gain supreme power as the Holy Roman Emperor.

There was thus an internal fight for the throne and a state of civil war, with the Turks just beyond the garden wall. Allegiances were shifting back and forth, the situation was totally confused, and at times everybody seemed to be against everybody else. Initially, John I was not doing well. His primary base of operations was Transylvania, that he knew well and that was far removed from Vienna and Prague, but here Ferdinand's men turned the Saxons against him. For a while he had to flee to Poland. He returned home with Turkish help or, perhaps, on Turkish orders, and took possession of the Hungarian crown. This demeaning alliance was barely sufficient for him to continue the civil war. The best he could achieve was to divide the country with Ferdinand along a line of demarcation. Even this had to be done in secret, in order not to offend the Sultan. Then, Ferdinand – underhandedly – leaked this information to Stambul, hoping to thus get rid of his Hungarian opponents. In Stambul, however, the Hungarians, having paid handsomely for this, stood higher than the Emperor. The Sultan was furious, but more with Ferdinand than with John. He forgave Szapolyai, but at a price.

What kind of a love affair was this between the national King of Hungary and Suleiman, who was a major threat to the freedom and independence of his country. It was not a love affair. John was quite conscious of the fact that his kingdom was at best a buffer zone. He was also convinced that the Habsburgs, being otherwise occupied, were not going to defend this peripheral area against gradual erosion by the Turks. Thus, the limited sovereignty offered by the Turks was the lesser of two evils. The price was an apparent – but nevertheless binding – loyalty to Stambul and the payment of a large cash tribute. Lesser evil, greater evil? A little of both... The decision that John had to make at this time on behalf of himself and of his country became a fundamental issue for Transylvania for many long years to come.

In the meantime, the multinational House of Fugger, utilizing all its pre-capitalism industry, tried to obtain the metal mining rights in northern Hungary, first from John and then from Ferdinand. They had been invited to do so, and then they had been forbidden the country. Most recently John granted them the rights to organize and exploit the mining and trading of salt in Transylvania. We know about this because one of their agents, a certain Hans Dernschwam who today would probably be described as their foreign manager, prepared a detailed travel and business report. On the 16th of August, 1528 he reported from Torda as follows: "In Torda we need draught horses, bridles, traces, steel, suet, heavy ropes, oats, hay, lumber, coal, hides, etc. All these things are unavailable but we can not function without them and must be aware of this. Thus, we have to pay double for everything and on the spot, since whoever goes to the market without much cash gets nothing. Everything should be bought in its own time, but since there are now no ready offers, we must buy everything at the worst possible moment. Everything needed for our work, food and all other necessities, must be obtained on a daily basis."

However, as he pointed out, to make money you need salt, but to get salt, you first need money. And so he continued: "I can't tell you precisely which road to use for bringing in money. The Abrudbánya road where you had such bad luck, is obviously not without danger. The Wallachians who did the robbery have become even more daring, since they have not been punished. If you want to use this road, you should do it only if you have armed mounted guards and if the carts have iron-shod wheels. The road toward Nagyvárad may be more open, but has not been used for a long time and may be a problem due to the Wallachians who live there. The people can be called to arms very quickly and they will then overrun the road. Without sufficient capital, the losses are going to increase. It would be best to bring it in along the Abrudbánya road. For protection, use some court officers, well supplied with letters of authority from the commanders and lords. Yet, if you think that it may be better, come directly here from Buda with a cart and a few horses. This would cause less commotion. The problems were actually initiated by the lords of the fortresses. One of the Wallachians admitted – before impalement – that he had acted on orders from Losonczy. The confession is with the judges at Brassó and Abrudbánya."

Who the Losonczy may be who was behind the Wallachian's crime was not given in the letter. Everybody looked only after their own affairs, the two kings and the Turks in their peculiar triangle.

Dernschwam tried to make all arrangements so that the country should have salt and – more importantly – that the Fuggers should make a profit from the salt. The lords fished in each others turbid waters, and the people engaged in robbery, by order or by individual initiative. All this, however, paled in comparison with the ongoing destruction caused by the various armies.

In the meantime, John Szapolyai acquired a wise friend and good counselor in the former soldier and current monk, the Croatian friar George Martinuzzi. Finally, he also got a wife, from Poland. Both of these facts will become more important after Szapolyai is gone. The "young" husband learned in July of 1540 that he had a son, and he wrote a testament accordingly. He died on July 17 or 21. On September 13, the ten-week-old infant was proclaimed king by the few nobles assembled at Rákos. He will use the name John II, but will never really be John II. Or will he?

It is now the summer of 1541. The young widow acted as regent in Buda, in the company of her son and his guardians. Buda was under siege and even many in Transylvania, not only the Saxons, are loyal to Ferdinand. The country resembled a multicolored mosaic, loyalties shifted back and forth and even Isabella was tempted to look toward Vienna for help against the Turk. Martinuzzi's primary purpose was to keep the Hungarians corraled under one flag. When he said anything else, he was playing political games.

It was the practice of the Turks to go campaigning every summer. In 1541, Suleiman again took the

road toward Hungary. He easily chased off the
Germans besieging Buda and then theatrically and
quasi paternally received the hopeful infant and his
entourage in front of his ceremonial tent. The verbal
promises of support were followed by an opulent
feast. While the feast was in progress, the Sultan's
janissaries wandered through the fortress of Buda
like friendly, familiar tourists. They liked it so much
that they decided to stay. In the evening, the Muezzin
called them to prayer from the tower, and the
Turkish emblem of victory, the horse tail flags, flew
from the battlements. – Just as it was supposed
to be.

"In exchange", Suleiman, at the foot of the Castle
Hill, graciously bestowed Transylvania, the area
beyond the Tisza and the Temesköz, on Isabella and
on the guardians of the infant. There was a very
modest annual tribute, but there were stringent
political conditions attached to the bequest. The first
of these was that Bálint Török, one of the three
guardians of the infant, and whom for reasons
unknown the Sultan did not trust, be delivered to
him. Török was taken as a captive to Stambul, and
after decades in the prison of the Castle of the Seven
Towers, died in captivity.

What began with the promenade of the janissaries
and with eastern effrontery, gives Stambul control of
the Carpathian basin. There will be fights, diplomatic chicanery, and more eastern tricks, but the Sultan
assumed the overlordship of the country in 1541.
Buda was not recaptured until 1686, almost a century and a half later. The reconquest was not accom-

plished by a ruse, but by a prodigious shedding of the blood of the united European armies.

The country, which consisted of two parts since 1526, is now divided into three. A large central triangle which extends well north of Buda and which includes the fertile Great Plains and the eastern half of Transdanubia, as well as the north-central mountains and the southern part of Transylvania became an increasingly integral part of the Ottoman Empire. The narrow western and northern area still belonged to the dynamic, but elsewhere occupied and fighting Habsburg Empire. The Austrian Hereditary Provinces formed a buffer zone against Turkish attacks toward Vienna, and a possible bridgehead for some future expansion toward the East.

What about the East? Friar George, who in the meantime received the scarlet hat of a cardinal, engaged in intermittent fights with the talented but very willful Isabella and desperately tried to maintain Transylvania on the shifting sands of international politics. He smoothed the path for Habsburg rule, since help from the west could come only from them, but he also had to stay on the right side of Stambul. Finally, with his assistance, Isabella and her son departed for Silesia, being compensated there with a minor principality. Martinuzzi seemed to reap his reward. While he was effectively governing already, he now ruled in the name of Ferdinand, who himself played a dual game. He gave complete control over the eastern regions to the Cardinal. Yet he cautioned his generals against him and secretly gave them full freedom of activity.

These were infernal times. Yet when did Transylvania have any other? The justifiably suspicious Sultan, partly for practice and partly to intimidate, repeatedly sent marauding parties into Transylvania, consisting of Turkish troops and Tatar, Serbian, Wallachian and other mercenaries. Learning about the removal of Isabella, he readied a general assault. Martinuzzi, who did not feel that his own Transylvanian forces, even combined with the troops of Ferdinand, were sufficiently strong, resorted to his usual tactical ploys, negotiated with individual pashas and tried to gain time. Considering this to be treason, he was killed in his castle by Ferdinand's commanders at the end of 1551. This proved to be worse than a sin. It was a mistake.

It was thus and here that the Transylvanian Principality was born from the blood of the friar. But not right away. The frontier fortresses fell, one by one, and the slow but persistent advance of the Turks was irresistible. Suleiman demanded the return of Isabella, which did occur in the fall of 1556. John II became king on the death of his mother in 1559, but really just in name. Weighed down by his inheritance, he makes a deal with Ferdinand's successor, the Emperor Maximilian (1564-1576), agrees to marry the emperor's daughter and cedes the inheritance to him in case the marriage did not produce a son.

Transylvania and Upper Hungary were riddled by betrayals and controversies. In 1562 there was a major Székely uprising and in the summer of 1566, John II had to go to pay homage to Suleiman in Zimony. The Sultan was on his way to Szigetvár, where he came to the end of his life. The death of Suleiman the Great and the ensuing interregnum gave a break to the Hungarian regions, but not to John. In 1571, the 31-year-old John Sigismund died. He had no children; in fact, he never married. How come? The reason was that he was so fond of his officer, councilor and friend, a certain Gáspár Békés, that he usually insisted that he spend the night with him, in the royal bedchamber.

These were infernal times. A contemporary song, quoted to me by a Transylvanian friend goes: "Prince John Sigismund / God, send us the Turks / Took my cow / To punish them / As tribute to the Emperor / Spare not their tribe / Beggaring me / Kill them where you can."

Who was here the emperor? In the final analysis, he was the one whose taxes were so mercilessly collected by John Sigismund's agents. No matter. Don't look at the precise words of the song, but at the split in personality, born of desperation. A people, in this case one of the Transylvanian nationalities, the Székelys called on the Turks, whom they know and dread, to take vengeance on their own masters. This was only one aspect of the period of John Sigismund, justly disliked by the Székelys. There was an other aspect, but first we must take a step back in time.

A Peculiar,
Peculiar Little Country

*I*t was only as recently as 1517 that Martin Luther nailed his theses to the door of the Wittenberg Cathedral. In the Transylvania of this time the yearning for a breath of fresh air in religion was not without precedent. The spirit of Hussism had reached northern Hungary directly, and hence Transylvania indirectly. Later some Anabaptists visited and then settled. Their descendants today are referred to as Habans on the basis of some of their pottery that has come down to us.

The Lutheran teachings found their optimal entry point simultaneously in northern Hungary and in Transylvania among the urban Saxon population driving for independence and for individual recognition. This trend was promoted by the fact that most of the early pathbreakers of the Reformation were Germans. Lutheran conversions among the Hungarians followed very shortly.

The first public religious debate was held in the Transylvanian Segesvár in 1538 between a Franciscan and a "Reformed" minister. It was not only condoned, but actually organized by John Szapolyai. (The outcome was a cautious "tie".) The Transylvanian Diet in Torda in 1548 wished to limit missionary ardor, but at the same time recognized

Lutheranism. This ordinance was classically two-faced and doomed to failure, yet it was undoubtedly elegant. The spread of the Calvinist form of Protestantism was also very rapid in our region. A 1557 edict of the Transylvanian Diet in Torda declared without any reservations that "Every one shall live in any religion of their choosing", while the remaining Catholics became persecuted minorities in some areas and were forced to move. They now had to be protected by laws.

We hasten to emphasize that this was not yet the end of the Catholic – Lutheran (Evangelical) – Calvinist (Reformed) chain. On this eastern edge of the Latin Christian world, the denial of the trinity, Anti-Trinitarianism also originating from the west, was deeply embedded and assumed the form of Unitarianism which evolved into a formal, national Church still very much alive today. Its evolution and flowering can be assigned to the era of John Sigismund, who at the end of his life was one of its followers. It is thus that in 1563, the Transylvanians – again at a Torda Diet – declared the freedom of the four "accepted" religions. These were: Roman Catholic, Evangelical, Reformed and Unitarian. The Eastern Orthodox creed practiced by the Romanians was not among the "accepted" religions, but the increase of both its wooden and stone churches and the functioning of its monasteries proves that religious tolerance extended to them. Their omission from the Torda decree was not due to religious causes but was a function of their societal –"national"– status.

The boldness and elegance in religious thought and religious life was relative and not entirely consistent. There were imprisonments and in some extreme cases even deaths connected to, or based on, enthusiasm in the propagation of various faiths. Yet the inquisitorial rage which, in the case of Servet, a noted Anti-Trinitarian, affected even Calvin himself, was entirely absent in Transylvania.

In Transylvania, the chain was not at an end even now. Dogmatically, Protestantism evolved primarily from a return to the text of the Scriptures. The Unitarians, even more radically, rejected everything that was post-Christ. One group in Transylvania based its entire reliance on the Old Testament alone. The Sabbatarians were getting close to Judaism, not only in the observance of the weekly holiday but in other religious questions as well. (Taking a giant leap in history, we must add that the Sabbatarians faced a dreadful end and that its members were caught up in the murder machine of the Holocaust of 1944. Their few survivors were welcomed in the new State of Israel).

In the middle of the above century, the increased religious freedom and the more liberal thinking that has led to it, the doubts and the ability to select one's path in life, also allowed the entire intellectual environment to flower and become much more colorful. The religious debates, occasionally bloody and rich in obscenities, led to significantly increased reading, translating, printing and publishing. The free exchange of ideas allowed many more young men from various classes in Transylvania to attend universities. Those returning from the universities introduced more up-to-date knowledge and teaching methods throughout the land. In this, the Protestants played a dominant role. Initially their endeavors were characterized by bringing religious and other novel ideas from abroad and by their dissemination at home. Later there was a vigorous exchange of religious and other ideas locally and by interpersonal contacts. The fame of the Transylvanian freedoms spread abroad. Protestants fleeing from persecution came in groups. Protestants in other parts of Europe welcomed the emancipated young men from Transylvania, celebrated for its religious innovations.

In the final analysis, much good and bad can be said about the Transylvania of John Sigismund. We must add that most of the bad things come from Székely tradition. For them the only thing by which they judged the man, who was the last national king and the first Prince of Transylvania, was that he drowned in blood their large scale and clearly justified rebellion, triggered by their increasing subjugation. They also bitterly resented that he had two new fortresses erected in 1562, primarily to control Székely activities. The one in Udvarhelyszék was called Székelytámadt (attacked by the Székelys), and the one in Háromszék was called Székelybánja (the Székelys regret it).

His successor had a totally different fate, way of life, perspective and historic reputation. Since John Sigismund died without issue, according to their agreement, Transylvania should have gone over to the Habsburg Maximilian. The nobles, fearing Stambul, and worried about their independence – a paradox, yet reality – preferred to elect István Báthori (1571-1586) as voivode. Following this challenging invitation, he secretly swore allegiance to Maximilian, while publicly accepting the endorsement of his election by the Sultan. His former gesture was in vain, he had to pursue Maximilian's adherents with armed forces. He reached the peak of his career four years later, in 1575, when in Cracow he was elected King of Poland. It appeared to the Polish electors that this little voivode from Transylvania may be more malleable in their hands than some of the other eligible candidates. If this was what they thought, they were wrong. Yet, they never had any reason to regret their decision.

This change of István Báthori's role was endorsed by the Turks as well, even though Báthori hoped that with this change he could gather enough strength to make a resistance to Stambul possible, or, at least, to be regarded as an equal partner by the Sultan. Just like Matthias Hunyadi, who first tried to protect his back and was recruiting a force, but never had an opportunity to attack in the south, István Báthori got into a bitter war with the Russian Tsar Ivan IV (The Terrible), and had all his future plans negated by his premature death at the zenith of his powers, at the age of fifty-three. He had no issue and his successor had no issue either.

According to Polish tradition, the decade of Báthori's reign is considered to be one of the glorious periods of their history. They are right. It was. At the same time, Transylvania was governed by Kristóf Báthori, the Cracovian king's honorable, but less outstanding elder brother as voivode. The fact that his activities were subject to a Transylvanian chancellery in Cracow can not be faulted, but his dynastic endeavors on behalf of his minor son are open to serious criticism.

Transylvania was kept in order and prospered under the long distance management of István Báthori. Under the rule of his nephew, the unfortunate Zsigmond Báthori (1588 -1599), the not inconsiderable political, moral and economic strength of the country was rapidly wasted. He was insecure, fled from responsibility, had a notoriously unhappy marriage, and intermittently resigned from and returned to the princely throne. Transylvanian memory recalls the last years of the old century and the first years of the new one as having been worse than the time of John Sigismund – no mean accomplishment.

The Habsburg mercenary troops, under the notoriously cruel Albanian general Basta, committed dreadful depredations in both men and goods, in spite of the fact that Zsigmond Báthori, leaving the throne for the last time, offered Transylvania to the very strange Emperor Rudolph (1572 -1608). We are going to give only one example of the many bad things that happened in this poor land, beset from so many sides. Transylvania became used to the idea that with the Turks on the other side of the fence, the Romanian voivodate of the Havasalföld, providing frontier troops for the Sultan, would make inroads from time to time. This, in itself, was not amazing. Such inroads were also made in the opposite direction. At this time, however, when the Turks were much less active in this region, Mihai, the Romanian voivode of the Havasalföld – the celebrated Mihai Viteazul, or Mihai the Hero who was born in 1557 and ruled from 1593 to 1601 – attacked Transylvania under Habsburg colors. For a short period he even became the ruling prince. It could not even come as a surprise that a number of Székelys, oppressed and rebellious under Zsigmond Báthori, were fighting in Mihai's army.

Two years and one year. This was all the time the next two rulers had. Yet, in the little time allotted to him, the very able military commander, István Bocskai (1605 -1606) accomplished much. He could do this because he managed to train a good army from among the previously chastised but now pacified Székelys and from the wild Heyduck. The latter, while not regular troops, could be disciplined fighting forces and they played an important and questionable role in the times to come. They became the cutting blades of a number of employers, which cut well, but could not rest. Condemned to inactivity – without pay or loot – they seemed to provoke new confrontations.

In the winter of 1604 -1605, Bocskai became successively the Prince of Transylvania and of Hungary, with the latter standing on the verge of having a national king. Located between "two great imperial powers", this astute soldier shied away from the kingdom. Being aware of his own military strength, he made a favorable peace with Rudolph, and he was the intermediary for a Turkish-Habsburg peace treaty. Death stopped him from enjoying the fruits of these endeavors.

While the several ambitious and mutually suspicious aspirants to the throne arranged a brilliant funeral for Bocskai in Gyulafehérvár, Zsigmond Rákóczi (1607-1608), having previously amassed an enormous fortune, had himself hastily and slyly elected as prince. Barely a year later he was dead. He was thus just an interlude, postponing the decision. His accomplishment was to bring another brilliant Hungarian magnate family to the fore. It will very soon have an enormous influence on the life and on the political power structure of Transylvania.

What a gallery! On the throne, the first one after Rákóczi was Gábor Báthori (1608-1613), the third member of this large family to hold this position. He was an eminent soldier, but an unbridled, avid lecher, and an insanely ambitious ruler. He attacked everybody and managed to antagonize everybody. The unfortunate result of this was that his behavior causes another shift in the Transylvanian political axis and that his former adherent and associate, Gábor Bethlen, was forced to seek increased Turkish contacts. The Sultan was also enraged and used his Turkish and Tatar troops to chase Gábor Báthori from his throne. This was not very proper, but was clearly indicated. Seeing that he had lost his political power, Báthori's Heyducks murdered him.

Let us interpose here something that really should have been discussed earlier, namely the actual form of government in Hungary and Transylvania. The House of Árpád, endowed with the crown under Stephen I, established an essentially unlimited royal government, where the succession was vested in inheritance and the legitimate king owed responsibility only to God. In actual reality and after much tug of war, there were increasing limitations placed on the personal power of the king and on the regulation of the succession. We must think only of the Golden Bull (the Hungarian Magna Carta), which instituted a form of social contract between the ruler and the ruled and which wrested concessions and promises from the ruler. After the reign of the House of Árpád, but particularly with the election of Matthias Corvinus and János Szapolyai, and contrary to the characteristics of absolute monarchy, Hungary and Transylvania functioned more like a republic of the nobles. The members of this "republic" naturally did not represent the entire population, but was largely limited to the higher and middle nobility. Gradually others were endowed with quasi noble attributes and were able to participate, directly, or through their representatives in gatherings which were now known as Diets.

This type of the republic of the nobility can be demonstrated in several Middle European countries. Here, a considerably larger percentage of the entire population is given noble or quasi-noble privileges than in the countries to the west of us where the classic feudal society limited the rule to a much smaller elite. To the east of us, the prevalent form of government was the absolute royal power, and the even more absolute despotism that prevailed for very many years to come. Even though there were geopolitical pressures, the decision to dethrone Gabor Báthori was made – with Turkish assistance – by the nobility. It was also their decision that made Gábor Bethlen (1613-1629) Báthori's successor. This was the beginning of Transylvania's Golden Age.

Transylvania in World Politics

A golden age? Why? How? The century in which the entire Carpathian basin had suffered immense losses in both men and goods had just come to an end. It is a well-known fact that demographic losses caused by warfare are rapidly made up by the surviving population. The dead and the captives are replaced by hastily conceived children. If, however, the losses caused by war are aggravated by losses caused by epidemics and natural disasters, the combined demographic losses may affect generations. The bill was further increased by the unrelated fact that in this era – the era of discoveries – the principal commercial routes had been redrawn. Also, bloody but cheap, the trans-oceanic gold and silver devalued the precious metal production and export in all of Europe and particularly in Transylvania and northern Hungary.

The literature on Gábor Bethlen's rule and personality fills libraries, and the interested reader can easily get lost in details. The early days of his reign – including the way in which he gained the throne – were overshadowed by the fact that he had to yield the fortress of Lippa to the Turks. Knowing how many fortresses have changed hands how many times, and how much the Turkish Empire has grown during these years, this one fortress does not seem to be of much importance. And yet, it was. The reason being that at this time there was a strong reaction against Bethlen's unpopular choice of leaning toward the Turks. And when on the Sultan's request, the prince, willy-nilly had to give up this important southern fortress, he had to besiege and evict his own troops who refused to give up the fortress. It was a terribly bitter lesson.

This took place in 1616. Two years later, Gábor Bethlen became involved in the first stage of the struggle between the rebellious Prague and the obscure Vienna, which spread throughout Europe and became the ebbing and flooding religious struggle known as the Thirty Years' War. The Counter-Reformation affected Transylvania only tangentially and its excesses were consistently rejected. Thus, Transylvania, strongly Protestant and with a strong Calvinist orientation participated in this war – one of the principal issues being man's freedom of choice – not as a minor, peripheral participant, but as a major player. At times, Transylvania became the most important player in this tragedy. Even though "the world" was expanding very rapidly in this age, and far beyond Europe, the role Transylvania had assumed in this struggle made it for the first and last time in its history a factor in world politics. After modest beginnings, this was no mean accomplishment for such a tiny country. Furthermore, at this very time, Transylvania enjoyed peace at home for the first time in a very long while.

"It was a peculiar characteristic of his armies that other than the regular tax, their existence did not weigh economically on the Transylvanians, who were pleased to hear about the successes of their prince in the far west without ever having to experience the fury of war on their own bodies. The life in Transylvania was like the mirrored surface of a lake, barely rippled by a gentle breeze, while the armies of the prince were engaged in bloody battles. Every barbershop in Pozsony was filled with the wounded and the dying and many regions of north and northwest Hungary became devastated battlefields year after year. In recent years these regions were also fighting a loosing battle with starvation. The sparse news reaching Transylvania caused very little excitement. All right, so the prince had again defeated the Germans or that this or that brave knight had fallen. This was nothing compared to the destruction of Transylvania in the decade following Zsigmond Báthori when the flower of the high nobility perished and the country was beset by five-six enemies at the same time (...) When the far distant prince requested additional men or increased taxes, the nobility gathered in National and County Assemblies, with the Saxons sitting in their own 'short meeting', regularly answered 'we will not give'. When a second request came, they promised to pay. Everybody knew that all this was incidental, that the prince waged war with his own resources and on his own responsibility and that he would abandon it when appropriate, having enough sense to judge the proper moment." (Gyula Szekfü.)

Gábor Bethlen was a good soldier, a statesman looking far into the future, a good master and a generous and wise patron. What Transylvania accomplished under his leadership is a witness, however, to the enormous potential strength of this land and of this people as well. "Just" a little calm, "just" a little order in its mercantile and administrative affairs, "just" a little enlightenment and toleration – with just enough Calvinist obligations in religious and lay matters – and, lo and behold, there emerged from behind the Habsburgs and from the shadow of the Turks a historically young, not very richly endowed, geographically limited, numerically small and so far – and soon again – fragile state. It will shine for a few decades with such a brilliant light, that it really would have deserved a more permanent favor from the fates.

It was Bethlen's intention to once again unite all Hungarians in one country. For this reason, he had himself elected king at the 1620 Diet in Pozsony. Unfortunately, he then lacked the strength to actually assume that position. His abdication from the kingly title gained him some territory. Then he tried to stabilize his position by marriage. Lastly, he attempted to gain the throne of Poland, like his predecessor István Báthori. All in vain. He helped others, nobody helped him. Or, if they eventually did, he did not live to see it. Thus, it was entirely in vain, both for him as an individual and also for Transylvania that during the first ten years of the Thirty Years' War, his armies were the only victorious ones and that during his life time his victories were instrumental in giving a breathing space to his German, English, Dutch and Danish allies.

At the time of Gábor Bethlen, Hungarian students ranged very widely and in large numbers to gain graduate and postgraduate education. In this laudable endeavor the sons of free peasants and even serfs, assisted with scholarships, accompanied the offspring of the highest nobility. Thus, the sons of the lower classes could rise in the social structure, thanks to Bethlen's generosity and to their own abilities. Previously, Hungarian names were found mostly in the student rosters of Italian, Cracowian and Gdansk universities, but now they appeared in German, Dutch and English universities, including Oxford and Cambridge. Gábor Bethlen established his own university. Surprisingly, his first such endeavor took place in the area of his military triumphs, in northern Hungary, in Nagyszombat, now in Slovakia. After lengthy wandering, this foundation became the Nagyenyed University.

After the death of Gábor Bethlen and after the interregnum and planned departure of the flighty and indecisive Catherine of Brandenburg, a new chapter of the story begins. Of the two hopeful young men, István Bethlen and György Rákóczi I – both of them having the Sultan's approval – the latter became the new prince (1630-1648). With him a well-known family of the highest nobility came to the top again. It is a family whose fate was intertwined more with Hungary than with Transylvania alone. Fate linked them to Hungary for several generations, and until the decline of the family. Otherwise conditions remained generally stable. There was some estrangement from Stambul, made possible by internal problems and dissensions within the Ottoman Empire. There was hope that the Thirty Years' War, dragging on and involving new participants, would take a favorable turn. There was another attempt to capture the Polish throne (this time with the help of the Cossacks rebelling against the Polish government, and for the favorite younger son of the ruling prince, Sigismund). There were some lucky victories in battle, great diplomatic skill, and considerable internal violence.

It was György Rákóczi's particular good fortune that he gained the hand of Zsuzsanna Lorántffy in marriage. She is the most outstanding example of Hungarian womanhood of that period. She was a helpmate in managing the estates, she was a patron of the schools and a benefactor of education, and she was the mother of four sons. At last we have a prince in Transylvania who had no dynastic worries. Let us not be too happy about this yet. Bad times were coming again to Transylvania.

Before discussing these, let us take a look at some of the characteristics of Transylvanian society in the middle of the 1600s. The increase in the estates of the prince did not affect the numerical relationships between the ruling classes and the others, but only within the ruling class itself. These latter were changed to the point where in the 13th century the prince was both the ruler and the landlord of "the majority of the Transylvanian serfs". For this reason, and contrary to other areas, "the peasantry fleeing from the shackles of serfdom could not look for protection to the State. The princes opposed the movement of serfs in all forms. They did not encourage the serfs if they wanted to enlist in the army or if they were looking for work in the mines. Even a move to crown lands was forbidden. The greatest severity, however, found it difficult to re-establish the bondage of the serfs, loosened by the destructive effects of fifteen years of war." (Katalin Péter.)

It is a paradox that at this same time the economic burden of the war became so heavy that the free Székelys who had fought so vigorously for the privileges granted to them by military service, sought the relative security of serfdom. The greatest guarantee of the Saxons' autonomy was their economic strength. This was supported for a long time by the fact that the Romanian voivodates, adjacent to Transylvania, were totally dependent on Saxon manufactured goods. When industrial productivity began in these voivodates, sufficient to meet their own needs, this destroyed the hitherto so lucrative eastern monopoly of the Transylvanian Saxons. The results were not purely economic, as far as the Saxons were concerned.

As far as the Romanians were concerned, their free peasants, lesser nobles and nobles and the sizable group of serfs were totally equivalent in position with their non-Romanian counterparts. If there was assimilation and Hungarization among the noble families of Romanian extraction – that was spontaneous and quite natural. The other segment of the Romanians, the mountain pastoralists were separate because of their way of life, their area of settlement and, most importantly, their mobility. Being short of serfs, the landowners attempted to move them down from their mountain grazing lands. When successful, their assimilation into the older Romanian serf groups was not harmonious. Their mentality differed too much and this meant more then the ties of consanguinity.

It is interesting that in the spiritual life of the Romanians there was little evolution of their native language, mainly because the majority of their clergy clung to the ancient Slavic liturgy. Thus, the refinements of the Romanian language were the triumph of a the small number of Romanian Protestants. This deserves more extensive discussion.

"The first important Romanian printed material was published in Transylvania under the influence of the Reformation. Princes, magnates and bourgeois, partly because of their enthusiasm for converting the Romanians, partly because of a sense of obligation to enlighten and educate, made a valiant effort to modify the thinking of the Romanians 'living in ignorance'. This effort was not motivated by Hungarian or Saxon nationalism. Starting with the 1540s, the Nagyszeben magistrate, the Brassó city judge, etc., show budgetary items dealing with the printing of Romanian religious books which were clear evidence of the attempts to create a Romanian literary language and a more modern religious life. (...) The Transylvanian, Romanian Reformed bishopric was established by the Nagyszeben Diet in 1566. It could not draw the Romanians away from Orthodoxy but made great strides in changing the language of the liturgy from the ancient Slavic to the native tongue (...). Conversion of the Romanians to the Protestant religion was again promoted by the great Transylvanian princes, Gábor Bethlen and

György Rákóczi I, with just as poor results as those of their predecessors. It is a fact that the orthodox counter moves tried to use the same tools and in the 17th century promoted the use of the mother tongue in the liturgy." (Zoltán Szász.)

Even today, Protestantism has been unable to put down roots anywhere from the northern Slavs to the southern Greeks. This very large area seems to foster a fundamental mentality among its various peoples, which does not favor trends which placed individuality in the fore front and encouraged the sovereignty of man.

György Rákóczi II (1648-1660) was picked already in 1642 by his very strong-willed father to succeed him on the throne. He took over his inheritance, free of any problems; a rare state of affairs in Transylvania. His reign started out well. He was helped by the realization that Protestantism had lost some of the "appeal" that it had at the time of his predecessors and thus he needed no longer be a champion of his religion. This made it easier for the majority of the western Hungarian, Catholic nobles, disappointed by the lack of resistance of the Habsburg against the Turks, to direct their hopes toward him personally, and toward Transylvania. This group included the outstanding soldier, organizer and poet Miklós Zrínyi, a scion of an eminent noble, Croatian family.

Time out! In 1643 György Rákóczi II married Zsófia Báthori, who had no male survivors in her own family. For his sake, she embraced Protestantism, but immediately following the death of her husband, she returned to Catholicism and also converted the successor Ferenc Rákóczi I, leading to major changes in the Rákóczi family...

In the first years of his rule, György Rákóczi II was fortunate to extend the influence of Transylvania to the Romanian voivodates. Matters may have progressed further in a favorable fashion, if his helpful and serious-minded younger brother Zsigmond had not died. This had fatal consequences. Taking advantage of the troubles in Poland, initiated and fomented by the Cossacks and relying on the promise of Swedish assistance, he pursued the plans of his father and started out with an army to conquer the Polish throne. He did this also, because the Turkish controlled areas of Hungary had increased to the point and were so firmly held that the road from Transylvania to the west necessarily led through Poland (this did not mean, however, that merchants and their goods could not cross all these areas in almost every direction). He should have known that he would not have Turkish support.

He also suddenly lost the Swedish support. The Poles did not view him as the reviver of the glorious Báthori era, but as a foreign aggressor. Indeed, why should they acquiesce in having a foreigner take the Polish throne with the assistance of Cossack and Swedish arms. In fact Polish armies operated far in his rear and plundered Hungarian territories. This induced the Cossacks to switch sides and, lastly – based on several historic precedents – Stambul sicked the Tatars on him as a disciplinary measure. He was forced to accept a demeaning peace agreement and had to pay enormous damages.

If, at this point, György Rákóczi quickly had turned around and took his intact army home, the losses would have been great but tolerable and recoverable. He did not realize, however, that good fortune had abandoned him, and he now committed the unpardonable sin. He and a few hundred of his soldiers "got out" and returned to Transylvania. His main forces, about 20,000 men strong were lured by the Poles into a Tatar trap. All of them were captured and were taken to the slave markets in the Crimea, where there was a real demand for human merchandise of such quality. He swore that he would use his entire fortune to redeem them and bring them home, but he did not do it.

Transylvanian – and Moldavian and Havasalföld – families were economically and emotionally destroyed by trying to get their relatives back from slavery. This endeavor created a brand new commercial and financial enterprise. To no avail. The majority of the slaves never returned home. The golden age of Transylvania was over.

The loss of the prince's reputation reflected unfavorably on the entire principality. During the next two years, György Rákóczi II was forced to abdicate twice and the succession, during his life, was chaotic and only temporary. In the meantime, Transylvania again became the battleground for both internal and external warfare. An extensive Turkish punitive campaign is estimated to have cost the life of 100,000 people. It can not serve as a belated excuse for his wasted life and for his very poor policies, that György Rákóczi II was wounded in the battle of

Szászfenes against the Turks and died from his wounds two weeks later.

Hungarian historiography, legitimately lists the son of György Rákóczi II, Ferenc Rákóczi I, among the princes of Transylvania, but without dates for his reign. Even though his father had him elected when he was six years old – just as he himself had been, by his father – the boy who is fifteen at the time of his father's death, could not in effect become the prince. His life and his fate were tied to his estates in Hungary and to his Hungarian political ambitions. It was there that he became a party to the Wesselényi conspiracy, it was there that his mother redeemed his life from Vienna, thanks to her strong influence among the Austrian Catholic clergy – and for an enormous ransom.

Four years after the fiasco of the Polish campaign and of the dissolution of the Transylvanian army in the Crimea, the Estates elected Mihály Apafi I (1661-1690) as the prince, on direct Turkish demands. He was of a meditative nature and, according to his contemporaries, more suitable for the priesthood than for the throne. His hobby – which he shared with other rulers at his time – was repairing clocks. He himself had been a prisoner in the Crimea and learned from this experience how the cogwheels of history meshed and ground. Reluctantly but inevitably, he bowed to the demands from Stambul. He did this for the time being only, since there was once again the hope and the possibility that Vienna, at long last, would exert its full strength against the Turk. It was a paradox of the situation, that his Turkish patron would be pleased to see Apafi on the

Hungarian throne. It was not the first time that a Prince of Transylvania was threatened with such a dubious distinction. The Hungarian kingdom was a shrinking remnant and once again, as so many times in the past, the question was whether the hated pagans could best be expelled by a Habsburg Vienna or by the re-establishment of a national sovereign. If the latter, a king must be found.

During these years, it is – again – difficult to follow in the Carpathian basin, as to who was fighting with whom, against whom and who was allied to whom. It all changed all the time. In 1664, thanks largely to the preparatory battles fought by that superb southern Hungarian nabob and Croatian governor, Miklós Zrínyi, Duke Raimondo Montecuccoli, a commander perhaps more celebrated than good, gained a great victory over the main Turkish forces at St. Gotthard. Yet Leopold I (1657-1705), Emperor of Austria and King of Hungary, made a hasty and almost demeaning peace with the Turks at Vasvár.

It is characteristic of the confused state of affairs that in Montecuccoli's victorious Christian army there were numerous French contingents, yet Leopold I made his disadvantageous peace with the Sultan, because he feared a sneak attack by the French. This peace enraged the Hungarian magnates and they, acting through the commander of the French expeditionary forces, offered military cooperation to Louis XIV against the Habsburg. Is it a wonder, therefore, if Mihály Apafi I also made inquiries from the Sun King from whom he got many promises and some money? His hopes were dashed, however, and Leopold made peace with the French. It was small solace, that in this peace treaty Transylvania was mentioned as an ally to the French. Transylvania thus, once again, albeit peripherally, appeared in world politics.

The East-Central European affairs, after a 150 years of spinning in place like a squirrel cage "between two pagans, for one country", finally gathered speed. In 1683, and for the last time, a Turkish army advanced against Vienna – not without troops from Apafi. In 1684, Apafi was invited by Leopold into an alliance against the Turk. In 1686, the allied forces of Europe evicted the Turks from Buda in spite of the fanatical fighting of the defending forces. Even though there would be Turkish remnants in various parts of Hungary for a while and some fortresses remained in Turkish hands for years rather than for months, the century and a half long, humiliating period in Hungary's history was at an end. It was near its end in Transylvania as well.

The most incomparable, famous and notorious figure of this age was Imre Thököly, twice prince without ever really being one. This great title was first bestowed upon him by northern Hungary in the first half of the 1680s. Later, in 1690, he was transiently Prince of Transylvania. In addition to his military prowess, that made him, deservedly, commander in chief of Transylvania at an early age, much of his fame was derived from his romantic marriage. He marries the widow of Ferenc Rákóczi I, Ilona Zrínyi, who was ten years his senior, and thus he became the stepfather of the minor Ferenc Rákóczi II. The Turks offered the Hungarian crown to

Thököly. He pretended to accept it, but never really claimed the title. We can view him as the last in a series of Hungarians who viewed the Turk as the lesser evil. Yet he wanted to remain "Turkophile" much longer than he could do so in good faith. Can this assessment be maintained after the events yet to come?

At the end of the century, the border between Christian Europe and the Islamic Sultanate was back again, generally in the same area where it was under the Hunyadis. How about Transylvania? Its situation changed, but it was a difference without a distinction. While it was a principality, it was the western border of an eastern empire (similarly to Hungary, after 1945 when, as a so-called "People's Democracy", it became the satellite of the Soviet Union). Now Transylvania became the eastern border of the Habsburg Empire which, although western, was loosing ground in the west and looked for compensation to the East, through the grace of God and for the greater glory of the dynasty.

Even though the principality was maintained for only a while, Mihály Apafi II (1690-1701) was still not the last prince. Leopold I, fully cognizant of his military superiority, reduces Transylvania to a status similar to that which the Turks had imposed on it in the past. He demanded an annual tribute. Every local decision was subject to the approval of Vienna. The Diploma Leopoldinum was issued on October 16, 1690, on demand by the Estates siding with the Emperor and was the "basic contract" integrating Transylvania into the Habsburg Empire. Its text has much to recommend it, it brought a bad period to its end, it did more good than bad, but it stayed in effect too long. In the meantime, Leopold I had the prince interned in Vienna, and finally reduced his status as a ruler to a simple territorial bargain. The weak Apafi heir was "compensated" with the title of Duke of the Holy Roman Empire, a meaningless sham.

This consistent curtailment of rights was not limited to Transylvania, so much so that instead of "Hungary", it would be more appropriate to speak of a "territory inhabited by Hungarians". According to Vienna, the expulsion of the Turks did not constitute a re-conquest. It was not the re-establishment of an earlier administrative status quo, interrupted by the Turkish occupation. It was a new military conquest, which was modestly referred to as a new acquisition and which thus was open to any kind of administrative arrangement. (*Nota bene*: a very significant percentage of the occupying army was Hungarian.)

The legal ruse was a clever one, but one thing led to another. Wherever despotism becomes the master – even if called military law – a strong hand and a strong saber are needed. Military governors are not generally known for their understanding, flexibility and spirit of cooperation. The generals appointed by Vienna proved to be particularly brutal. Looting and the imposition of tributes may be ancient military prerogatives but they did little to pacify the "liberated" who hoped that the liberation would result in freedom after the expulsion of the Turks.

The activities of General Antonio Caraffa in northern Hungary and Transylvania were successful for

Leopold I only in the short range. He "pacified" the occupied territories and incorporated them into the Empire, but he sowed seed that would soon grow into bloody shoots. We could begin the story of the last Prince of Transylvania at this point.

On the other hand, this period is noted for people in hiding. We may even call them "internal emigrants". Since 1514 there were many fallen rebels, military deserters, escaped serfs, displaced peasants, returning prisoners of war who had lost their homes, people banished from a party, movement or religion, unemployed cattle drovers and journeymen, miners dismissed for striking, escaping felons and others, who were banding together in the swamps and forests in increasingly large numbers and more and more openly. Some of those who had formed regular groups have already been mentioned under the designation of Heyducks.

This is another point in our history where we can begin the story of the last Prince of Transylvania. Even though Ferenc Rákóczi II (1704-1711) was the fifth member of his family elevated to this dignity, his childhood star was pointing in a different direction. As a stripling he was in a military camp with his step-father, Imre Thököly, and he was there when his mother fought for three years with the imperials to defend Munkács. After the loss of Munkács, the youngster was educated by the Jesuits, who functioned almost like prison guards – his patrimony of one million hectares would have been a nice acquisition for the Order. He was deeply religious, but as soon as he reached majority he left this forcibly imposed guardianship. Marrying soon thereafter, he moved back to northern Hungary in 1694 and immediately became the great hope of the national resistance. At this time, however, he avoided all political obligations. The successfully initiated Hegyalja Peasant Rebellion of 1697 invited him to become its leader. He was so scared that he ran all the way to Vienna. Yet the miserable conditions in the country, recently liberated from the Turks, and the brutal reprisals against several popular movements shook him severely and initiated a slow transformation.

Let us remember: some of his ancestors were Princes of Transylvania when it was the glorious bastion of Protestantism. He himself was the child of the Counter-Reformation. His maternal great grandfather was the hero of Szigetvár, his uncle was the poet and military theoretician Miklós Zrínyi, his grandfather, Péter Zrínyi, was lured to Vienna with false promises and was there subjected to the executioner's blade. These are just a few items of the many that shaped his fate. In 1701, the recently begun War of the Spanish Succession created a favorable atmosphere and he began to send out feelers toward Paris. He was now ready for a leadership role.

The always suspicious Vienna swept down on him. He was carted off, threatened with the death penalty and escaped only with a romantic trick and at the price of his liberator's life. He hired mercenaries in Poland and got ready to return to his country, but the leaders of the newly exploding popular rebellion had already sent for him. Very soon the country was in flames from east to west. The light cavalry troops of the Kuruc captains now fought under Rákóczi's flag and swept down on the fragmented imperials, all the way to the gates of Vienna.

The Prince-Commander, who was elected to this dignity after the initial successes of the Kuruc movement, first by the Transylvanian and then by the Hungarian Estates, depicted contemporary Hungarian society with astonishing maturity. His writings are filled with Christian meditations, but they also contain an almost sociological analysis of the class structures and of the impediments to his struggle created by the societal immaturity and by the general backwardness of the country. Yet, combining the revenues of the state and of his own estates, he created an effective war economy and a monetary system which could function with minimal backing – as long as he had the "golden touch" of victory in battles.

He had two problems, however, which were insoluble. He builds good contacts at the two opposite poles of Europe with Louis XIV and with Tsar Peter the Great, but as soon as the international situation changed it was no longer in the interest of either France or Russia, that this little Hungarian princeling "annoy" Vienna. The other issue was that the real strength of his army rested on the rebellious poor, the barefoot axe and scythe bearers, the *talpas* – they included numerous nationalities and the particularly faithful Carpathian Ruthenians – the Heyducks and the serf-soldiers fighting for their freedom. Rákóczi recognized this and tried to draw the appropriate legal conclusions. Yet, he was dependent upon the magnates and nobles whose interests were the opposite. He was their prince.

From 1703 to 1711, the war was like a kaleidoscope with a shifting base and alternating losses and gains. Once again Hungarian confronted Hungarian: the Labanc included a number of Hungarians who preferred Vienna.

The last few years were a series of pursuits and hairbreadth escapes for the Kuruc forces. Their ranks were thinned by desertion and weakened by epidemics. The noble estates were short of serfs and the economy was destroyed by the now worthless coinage. Rákóczi was forced into exile. He refused the offered amnesty and the German estate offered in exchange for his own. He fled to Poland. He met Peter the Great. Then he went to France where he was first the popular, romantic hero in the colorful entourage of the Sun King, and later lived in monastic solitude like a friar.

It gave him satisfaction that the Peace of Szatmár which he did not oppose, granted many of the things that he could not gain on the battlefield. The re-establishment of the legal status of Hungary and Transylvania, which had been wiped out after 1688 on the basis of military law, became the subject of complicated bargains and later unkept promises. Religious freedom was re-established, and the Heyducks maintained their privileges. It was less satisfactory that the nobility, taking advantage of the amnesty kept its privileges by taking a step backward historically. It was a paradox that now – and also at other times – Vienna having gained a free hand, promoted modernization in the Carpathian basis in opposition to the conservatism of the nobility.

In 1717 Ferenc Rákóczi moved to Turkey, like his late mother and stepfather before him, hoping for support from the Sultan. Unfortunately, the international situation was unfavorable. He was assigned a small town, Rodosto (now Tekirdag), on the shores of the Marmara as his domicile. He lived there with his few remaining faithful, on a small stipend from the Sultan, until his death in 1735.

This is the end of the chapter that we dared to call Transylvania in World Politics. What we meant by this was that in this era, the distant and exotic land "beyond the forests", previously unknown in Europe, became useful in transient power blocks, was considered a useful potential ally and actually served as a useful ally in some situations. At no time thereafter did it participate in similar "glory". Not even when, like in the 20th century, it repeatedly became a bargaining chip in world politics. At this time it was only a minor appendix of Hungary or Romania, and was not a (relatively) independent factor.

Cast onto the Periphery

*E*ven though we had accompanied Ferenc
Rákóczi II on his final exile, we must take a step
back in time. He was the last Prince of Transylvania,
but the fate of Transylvania was not the stake in his,
for him fatal, fight for freedom of glorious memory.
Neither was it the patient Transdanubia, the devastated Great Plain or the Small Plain close to Vienna.
The stake was the Felvidék and northern Hungary,
which was in a peculiar position during the Turkish
occupation, having an intermediate situation and
taking and extorting all possible advantages of this
situation. It was this area that furnished the armies of
Rákóczi with a high percentage of enthusiastic and
important followers.

It was never the strategy of the rising to first
cleanse Transylvania of the imperials and then to
continue the war by slowly advancing from east to
west toward Vienna. One reason for this was that a
significant part of the costs of the war had to be furnished by the Rákóczi estates, most of which were
in Upper Hungary. The indications and moral basis
for the rebellion, stated by Rákóczi frequently in
manifestoes and also in his memoirs, were not the
oppression and the yearning for freedom of the

"three nations" of Transylvania, but of the entire Hungarian nation.

It has been mentioned that from the time of the conquest to the incursion of the Turks into the Carpathian basin, it became an accepted fact that there were going to be regional divisions. Yet, Transylvania was a fundamentally Hungarian conquest and settlement area and was an organic part of the Kingdom of Hungary, founded by and incorporated into the realm under the "holy" crown. In this spirit, the separate Transylvanian principality did not originate from any internal Transylvanian demands, but were imposed by external circumstances and the consequences of the disaster of Mohács.

We must assume then that the House of Habsburg, having obtained the royal crown of Hungary – legitimately according to its own legal theories, was anxious to place Transylvania under the sway of the Crown as soon as possible. Not so. Vienna was successful in convincing Mihály Apafi II to exchange his Principality of Transylvania for a German Imperial Dukedom. Ferenc Rákóczi rejected a similar offer. When Vienna no longer had to be concerned with a Prince of Transylvania, or with pretenders for this title, it still viewed this distant province as a border buffer zone and attempted to control it as a separate entity, directly subject to the Imperial Crown. It was willing to assume the burden of a separate administration and the bother and labor of dealing with the local nobility in matters of governance and law. Thus, they could further divide and manipulate this "Eastern" nation: the Hungarians, using regional interests as a lever.

The legal bargaining soon assumed a special significance. It happened in 1711 that due to the unexpected death of his brother, Charles Habsburg, was summoned from his very shaky Spanish throne to the other end of the family empire. As King of Hungary he was Charles the Third, while as Holy Roman Emperor he was known as Charles the Fourth. He was the last male member of the previously, and again in the future, so fertile House of Habsburg (1740). Charles made early efforts to assure that the dynasty continue through its female branch. This was why he proclaimed the Pragmatica Sanctio in 1713, and had it accepted in 1722, first by the Transylvanian Estates, and then by the Hungarian ones. For the first ones, he used a trick and the Diet was not only very poorly attended but was held in the Saxon town of Nagyszeben.

One might ask why Vienna made such consistent efforts to increase its hold on Transylvania, other than the insatiable greed for additional territory which characterized the dynasty. Even though the importance of the gold and silver mines had decreased, they were still important. Even more important were the salt, copper and mercury. More important than any of these, however, was the fact the Turk still lurked beyond the "garden wall". He was a live threat. What if he again became active? His expulsion from the Balkans was inconceivable unless the flanks were properly protected. It was this strategic consideration which explains the diligence with which the Austrian Emperor – again, primarily through its military forces – protected and increased his control over Transylvania. The Empire even endeavored to expand beyond the Carpathians.

. This will be beneficial for Transylvania. It is true that after having gotten used to navigate well in the ebbing and flowing waters of its dependence from the Turks, it now had to adapt to the more rigorous, closed system of a more rigidly centralized government. Its bureaucracy, trying to establish order and usually warding off arbitrary autocracy, at times was as cruel as the "barbarian" pashas. Fortunately, in the times to come, the direction of the campaigns was being changed. The still paramount anti-Turk military maneuvers were shifted to the south and east of Transylvania, much to everybody's relief.

The ethnic composition of the population at this time was estimated to be: Hungarian 45-50 percent, Romanian 30-40 percent and Saxon 10-15 percent. Of these, the lower numbers were probably the more correct ones in view of the several other nationalities not included in the list. There was also a constant movement of people. Its main direction was east to west. Many settled individually in the territories vacated by the Turks. Others were transplanted from Transylvania by magnates having depopulated estates farther west. This created a vacuum, and the shortage of people in Transylvania was being replenished by the entry of Romanians from beyond the Carpathians. This migration was both spontaneous and organized and further shifted the ethnic balance.

Protestantism remained strong and the rights of the Protestants were always an important issue in the political bargaining with Vienna. A new element was that the previously forcefully Catholicizing

Vienna now was trying to convert the Greek Orthodox Romanian population to the more "intermediate" Greek Catholic Church. It made many promises to the clergy and offered privileges withheld from the Orthodox priests. These obvious attempts of assimilation and the Pravoslav reaction with its nationalistic overtones was the source of conflicts, lasting to this day, and involving areas beyond those inhabited by Romanians, such as the Ukraine and Eastern Slovakia.

It is of considerable interest, beyond its purely technical considerations, that the Transylvanians of the 18th century took advantage of the favorable geographic and hydrographic conditions and used the water-wheel not only for milling grain, crushing ores and driving lumber mills, but for many other purposes as well. The altitude and the hard winters limited the ingenious use of water-power to seasonal use.

Even though local mining and smelting made iron readily available, the water-driven machines were largely constructed of wood with minimal iron reinforcements. The Transylvanians, but primarily the Székely men, were masters of all wood working and carpentry and are so even to this day. Mastery of wood working obviously had no ethnic limitations, but it was axiomatic that the Székely way of thinking, their inventiveness and cleverness were frequently manifested in the development of complicated gadgetry. Today, when we are so concerned with man's exploitation of his nurturing environment, we seek for the historic roots of ecological thinking, of the recognition of the problem and of endeavors to correct it. Newer studies have found rich source material for these issues in the old Székely village ordinances. It is worthwhile to quote from the 1733 village ordinances of Papolcs in County Háromszék: "Since our stream, which gives us life, is usually small during the summer, in consideration thereof, nobody dare dispose of any household dirt, dung and, particularly dead animals in or near said water. The furriers and tanners shall not soak any hides nor pelts nor hemp above or below the village in the running water. Not above or in the village for fear of dirtying the drinking water and not below the village for fear that the substances placed into the stream to soak may dam up the flow and produce floods to the great detriment of the people. Hemp soaking ponds may be established in certain locations by anybody, but nobody dare establish such ponds to the hazard and detriment of the village, its, roads, mills, etc."

This rather attractively worded ordinance testifies not only to the fact that the Székely village recognized its dependence on nature and tried to prevent its pollution, but also that the peasant population realized that ordinances for the common good could be codified internally by the village community.

It is of interest to the writer that a similar conscientious, responsible local codification took place in the early 1600s in his native area, in the small boroughs and villages of the grape-growing and wine producing Tokaj-Hegyalja district. These ordinances dealt primarily with property matters, inheritance, acquisition of new property and economic matters – trade, lease, taxation – that is, with the relationships between man and man, rather than with issues between man and nature.

When now – toward the middle of the century – it became obvious that there was no possibility for a Rákóczi restoration with or without Turkish assistance, and no chance for the re-establishment of a Transylvanian principality, the attempts of Charles Habsburg to have the Pragmatica Sanctio accepted became very reasonable. In the absence of a male heir, he was followed on several of his thrones by his daughter, Maria Theresa (1740-1780). From a Hungarian perspective, her reign was a mixed blessing. Sometimes it was beneficial, sometimes it was harmful.

The evident economic upturn and the lasting agricultural prosperity, which was very beneficial to Hungary, seems to have stopped at the western borders of Transylvania. Here the agricultural opportunities were slimmer, the distances were great and the modern methods of agriculture developed only gradually. The growth of the cities and the urbanization of the population, so noticeable in the past, had slowed down. There was insufficient economic backing for it. The commerce and industrial production improved to some degree only when the Romanian principalities beyond the Carpathians gained strength and became important markets.

It was during the 30s and 40s of this century that the national ideas and trends of the numerically and educationally improving Transylvanian Romanians appeared. This group, which represented a third of the population, wished to have itself accepted as the fourth Transylvanian nation. It wanted the appropriate rights and privileges, if for no other reason, than by ancient rights. It was in this period that the hypothesis of the Daco-Roman Continuity appeared. It will cause much debate and even more controversy.

Its founding father was the leading bishop of the Unitus, meaning those united to Rome – i.e. the Greek Catholics, one Inochentie Nicu-Klein (1635). This young, dynamic and educated prelate, who was a clever tactician, was relying on the promises made and benefits granted by Leopold I to the Unitus. Even though these were religious concessions, he wanted to use them to give all Romanians, including the peasants, a new standing in law. In doing so, he would also gather in the Orthodox. Vienna slowly and carefully makes concessions to him for the reason – which he did not appreciate – that these concessions were made at the cost of the other Transylvanian people and particularly at the cost of the Hungarian nobility.

The fact that the raising of these novel Romanian national interests were intertwined with the interests of the peasantry and with the emphasis on the backward state of the mountain shepherds and of the peasant-serfs gave it its real significance. Nicu-Klein linked their case to the entirely different kinds of priorities and endeavors of the other Romanian classes and also to the manifold, colorful mythical threads of the ideological theories of Romanian national identity. At the famous and often cited Balázsfalva Assembly, which he called together in 1644, even though it was nominally a religious synod, it was the practical, rather than the ideological side of the issues which came to the fore. Actually it may be misleading to call this synod-assembly practical, when it declared that the active participation of the people may be highly commendable, but at this time it was not yet realistic.

Paradoxically, the greatest and most damaging opposition to these early Romanian national aspirations came not from Vienna or from the other opposed nationalities, but from the Orthodox counterattack against the spreading Greek Catholicism. This Orthodox resistance was fomented partly by the Serbs, but more forcefully by Russian religious and political interests. Austria still needed Russian support in the War of the Austrian Succession, which was due to the Pragmatica Sanctio being far from universal acceptance. For this reason, Vienna temporarily stopped supporting "their" Unitus and made concessions to the Orthodox Romanians. The latter, wishing to be helpful, became even less supportive of the burgeoning Romanian national ideas. Later on the role of the two religious denominations was reversed. Inochentie Nicu-Klein himself, after much persecution found asylum in the Vatican and observed from there the atrophy of his initiatives and of the respect that he once held.

Beyond the mid-point of Maria Theresa's rule, the generals of the Austrian army gained increased prominence; it can be said that Transylvania became the testing ground of an overt military dictatorship. The whole system of border protection was reorganized. Of the newly recruited border forces, half were Romanian. Service was very onerous and thus – as Vienna had hoped – few volunteered. Yet, for the Romanians in the army, it first promised and then meant social advancement and led for the first time to the public education of their children.

The Székelys, who were the "born border guards", were very pleased to learn about the reorganization of the service, provided this would lead to the re-establishment of the so often curtailed and reduced Székely military and border guard privileges. They wanted to serve in their own units and under the command of Székely officers. The proposal by the Austrian militarists, namely, forced enlistments, foreign regulations and foreign commanders, may have been beneficial for the Romanian peasant-serfs, but induced the majority of the free Székelys to escape. Where to? They withdrew to their mountains and forests. When the unhappy Székelys of County Csík assembled in Mádéfalva, a certain General Siskowicz interpreted this as an uprising and surrounded them with his troops at dawn on January 7, 1764. It was not a fight. It takes two to make a fight. What happened was a massacre that left several hundred dead. The Mádéfalva tragedy was a blow to the entire Székely community from which it has never fully recovered. They have gone through many perils, but it was Mádéfalva that made the "People of Prince Csaba" realize their depressing historic defenselessness.

The events of Mádéfalva left tragic traces not only in the Székely national soul. They also increased the emigration which again and greatly replenished the Hungarian and Székely settlements in Bukovina. These Moldavian Csángó and Bukovine Székely settlements had a most sorrowful fate, and some of them subsist in heart-rending misery to this day.

The distance separating Transylvania economically from Central Europe and even from the western parts of Hungary was less noticeable in the cultural arena. The linkage systems in intellectual and scholarly life functioned, even though at times under considerable difficulties. The Protestants maintained their contacts with their traditional Western European partners. Transylvanian students continued to study at foreign universities. Transylvanian educators maintained an active correspondence with the colleagues they had met during their study years. The Saxons who created a separate German culture in Transylvania were a true, albeit peripheral, part of German culture. The international nature of the Catholic religious orders was strengthened by the Counter- Reformation, and was well recognized. The Romanians were necessarily somewhat in the rear of the cultural mainstream, and it was primarily the Unitus priesthood that had the opportunity for more information. A number of them had studied in Rome. The linkage of the Orthodox priesthood to Greece and Russia was – contrary to the views and writings of Romanian historians – a negative influence. On the other hand, the number of well trained Romanians achieving official positions in Transylvania continued to grow, and their further advancement and options were determined by their position, and not by their nationality.

The decades of Maria Theresa – and even more so the years of Joseph II (1780-1790) – were characterized by a Germanizing trend and by a centralized, rational government. It is a paradox that in Transylvania this centralization, with its merciless unification and more advanced and thus more intrusive administration, was most damaging to the Saxons, since they had established and maintained an autonomy that was inevitably curbed by centralization. The new administration reaching out to the individual, clearly made any concerted societal activity much more difficult. The Romanians were the greatest beneficiaries. Central control diminished the chances of their being exploited, and public education decreased their lagging behind.

In 1711, the Peace of Szatmár referred to it, in 1740 Maria Theresa – under duress – confirmed it. Transylvania was part of the Hungarian Crown, directly as a principality. We have seen, however, that Vienna tended to separate the administration of Transylvania and it was only during the last years of Maria Theresa's reign that the pendulum began to swing back toward administrative unification. The customs barrier between Transylvania and Hungary was eliminated by Joseph II, and it was this action that again made the Carpathian basin into an economic unit after a long period of time. Being on the periphery was beneficial to Transylvania – and to northern Hungary – at this time. Vienna, in order to protect Austrian and Moravian industry, actively prevented the development of manufactories west of the Lajta, which would convert a cottage industry into a mass production industry. At the periphery, the local officials could tacitly condone such developments, or they may have proceeded covertly.

Maria Theresa and Joseph repeatedly tried to regulate socage and serfdom itself. This was being made very difficult by the stubborn resistance of the nobles and by the bureaucracy and inexperience of their own administrative apparatus. In spite of the enormous differences in their personality – the mother had empathy and patience, the son was forceful and impatient – the results achieved by both were inconclusive. Also, the further from the Centrum from where the imperial urging and mandates came, the greater the public resistance and the splintering and fading of the original intent of the mandates.

Joseph II and Josephinism are as suitable to a novel as they are to history. His almost utopian, enlightened absolutism was overshadowed, even for the few Hungarians advanced enough to understand it, by the fact that the "Uncrowned king" (the King in the Hat) considered progressiveness to be purely Germanic. He alloyed progress with a comprehensive Germanization but gave it a fatal blow with the retractions he made on his deathbed. He suffered one of his painful disappointments in Transylvania.

What was it that triggered the bloody Horea serf rebellion of 1784? While the Court wished to curb the excesses of the landowners by regulating the burden of the serfs, locally there was a complicated system of tacit agreements, so that unification and better record keeping actually increased the burdens in some areas and "cast them in concrete". In matters affecting the serfs, those affected equated regulation with liberation. It could easily be viewed as a sign of weakness, and became the source of further demands. At the same time, a new and poorly executed recruiting effort further agitated Romanian public opinion. They expected opportunities and privileges from the enlistments that the recruiters had not actually promised. The whip and the club landed on the masters who were naturally Hungarian, although not necessarily to the seventh generation. It is probably not justified to highlight this rebellion over other similar popular uprisings, except perhaps for the violence and counter-violence of some of its excesses, such as the forceful marriage of Hungarian noble maidens by Romanian "suitors". These gave it wider renown than would be deserved either by the numbers involved, or by the geographic extent of the rebellion. Its origins were actually more societal than national.

One of the first acts of Leopold II (1790-1792) on his succession to Joseph II, was to swing the pendulum in the other direction, and once again separate Transylvania from Hungary. It succeeded only partially, even though the endeavor was not totally opposed even in Transylvania. The Protestants were concerned that in case of a union, their rights would be curtailed. The Saxons and the Székelys were opposed for similar reasons. In the meantime – and even though Joseph II's death did not end Josephinism, which was a synonym for practical absolutism – the Estates requested that the Transylvanian Diet be called into session.

It not only met, but passed a number of acts. "The Transylvanian Diet began its work on December 21, 1790. Its minutes are frighteningly voluminous and its additional documentation fills a freight car, documenting that it had indeed very much to do. The scribes could barely keep up with the memoranda, petitions and supplications all of which were filled with complaints, offenses and, naturally, demands.

The documents of the Diet can very clearly tell the modern reader exactly where Transylvania stood in relation to the general European developments, what it was that the literate people of this small country could absorb from the general storehouse of enlightenment and the directions – political, economic and intellectual – in which it tried to move. Among the papers we find the famous Supplex Libellus Valachorum in which the Transylvanian Romanians requested that they be acknowledged as the fourth nation and be given autonomy as a recognized Estate." (Samu Benkő.)

The sessions lasted well into the new year, and made many decisions and submissions but, in the end, achieved very little. Making our language the official one took a step forward with the decision that the minutes of the Diet be kept in Hungarian. The rights of the serfs and of the Orthodox had been enlarged. A proposal was made for the establishment of the Association for the Propagation of the Hungarian Language in Transylvania, which assumed the nature of an academy when it began its activities three years later.

The Supplex Libellus Valachorum, which was prepared by a large but still not completely known circle of Romanian priests and other intellectuals, based the Romanian demands it contains both on the Theory of Daco-Roman Continuity as its ideological-historic argument, and on the popular majority of the Romanians in Transylvania as its concrete demographic and statistical argument. There is nothing we can do with the former one, but the latter one cannot be denied. At this time the Romanians represented the largest ethnic group in Transylvania. Yet, they were the last, both in their legal and in their economic status. In order for them to change this, the differences between the Unitus and the Orthodox had to be reduced.

The answer of the Estates was that regardless of their serfdom, nobility or other status and regardless of their ethnicity, all inhabitants of Transylvania had the same rights. What else could one want? It cannot be denied that this "slippery" argument haunts even today, for instance, in the Romanian rejection of the national and minority demands of the Transylvanian Hungarians. The argument of the Estates continued by saying that the problem of the Romanians was not lack of liberty, but lack of education. This should not be considered an insult, particularly not when we consider that the Transylvanian Hungarians, noting the narrowness of their own legal and political perspectives, made great efforts to improve their educational opportunities. The first permanent home of Hungarian theatrical performances was opened in Kolozsvár in 1821. The strong links with Europe were also demonstrated by the rapid spread of Freemasonry. Its principles started to spread in 1742, first to the Saxon cities, and then to the circles of the Hungarian leading classes.

The functioning of the Freemason lodges over the next decades was first banned, then tolerated and finally almost supported. We may even assume that the strange Joseph II himself was granted membership. Not so. He wrote in a letter of instruction: "Previously and in other countries the Freemasons were punished and their meetings in the lodges were disrupted only because they were not familiar with their secrets. Even though these secrets are unknown to me as well, it is enough for me to know that these Freemason lodges have done much good for friendship, for the relief of want and for education. I hereby order, that even though their by-laws and discussions remain unknown to me, they be granted the protection of the State and that their meetings be permitted as long as they continue to act beneficiently. This is more than was done for them at any time and in any other country." The conditions laid down subsequently were fairly strict, but there is no doubt that the permission, quoted above, was liberal and elegant.

Those organizations which were devoted to the propagation of the Hungarian language, scholarship, public education and literature were less fortunate, even though they were not surrounded by the secrecy of freemasonry. The suspicions of the authorities were not without some foundation. For instance, in the Diana Hunting Society, organized in 1794 by the noble reform groups, there was less talk about the very popular hunts in Transylvania than about agrarian problems and about the importance of an interchange in social activities between the lesser, middle and highest nobility. This was also the time when the effects of the Hungarian Jacobin movement became evident in Transylvania. It was fortunate for the Transylvanians that these effects were not due to a direct association, but rather just to the indirect, intellectual transmission of ideas.

The Habsburg Empire of Francis I (1792-1835) was slowly eroded by the enormous external forces weighing on it. It was during his reign that his aunt, Marie Antoinette, was beheaded in Paris. Yet later he had to give his daughter to Napoleon, who not only was the principal beneficiary of the blood-soaked French revolution, but was an upstart and a divorced man. This happened only three years before the Little Corsican lost the fateful battle of Leipzig, and only five years before the battle of Waterloo put an end to his brief return to power. Thus, the Austrian self-debasement accomplished very little. These few lines suggest that at this time the important events took place far from Transylvania. Francis I, as King of Hungary, shifted back and forth. His inclination was toward a show of force, such as the execution of the leaders of the tragic Hungarian Jacobin movement. Yet, he needed Hungarian soldiers and Hungarian money so much, that he was willing to make certain concessions.

Bright stars appeared at this time in the heavens above Transylvania. About the turn of the century a lesser noble youth walked home all the way from Göttingen. It was the mathematician Farkas Bolyai (1775-1856) who kept up a correspondence with his former student friend, Karl Friedrich Gauss, who was later known as the prince of mathematicians.

In 1819, the Székely Sándor Kőrösi Csoma (1784-1842), looking for the ancient home of the Hungarians, started out toward the East, also on foot. He reached Tibet and having suffered deprivations that would have done justice to a fakir, he gathered linguistic material and wrote the first Tibetan grammar and the first Tibetan-English dictionary.

The son of Farkas, János Bolyai (1802-1860), was a military engineer and mathematician. In parallel with the above mentioned Gauss and the Russian genius Nikolai Ivanovich Lobachevski, and far outstripping the traditional mathematical thinking, he worked out the non-Euclidean "complete" or "absolute geometry" of which Euclidean geometry was only a special facet. Avoiding the unrewarding arguments about precedence, one must admit the originality and the great individual contributions of the three men. One must mention, however, that in his notes János Bolyai almost fully recognized the general theory of relativity which evolved from non-Euclidean geometry, but which was only fully developed, and published, by Einstein. In this, Bolyai was far ahead of his time.

Kőrösi Csoma and the younger Bolyai were two Transylvanian geniuses in touch with the science of their days, but who labored much more in isolation than their more fortunate western contemporaries, and who produced such intellectual achievements under such unfavorable conditions that it can be compared only to the lustrous pearl born from the sufferings of a wounded oyster.

Transylvania had not suffered the direct ravages of war for a long time. Epidemics were less frequent, public health was improving. The population increased rapidly, but the Saxons and the Hungarians, less likely to become urbanized, fell behind. The Romanians forged ahead. The region was agriculturally not self-sufficient. The cereals used in baking were imported from the Banate and from the Great Hungarian Plain. They were paid for primarily in wool and in the products of the mines. It is of interest that it was still under Maria Theresa's maternal rule that the potato was introduced into Transylvania. Its wide distribution was forcefully demanded by the central administration wishing to benefit the people. At the same time, corn, which very rapidly became an enormously important component in the nutrition of the people of Transylvania and quite particularly among the Romanians, was discouraged as being detrimental to the productivity of the lands producing cereal grasses.

The 19th century entered its second quarter. It was the beginning of the Reform Age, which will resound with the debate between the more careful and remote István Széchenyi and the more radical and trouble making Lajos Kossuth. This reached Transylvania in its relative isolation, even though one of the greatest figures of this age, Miklós Wesselényi, was more of a mentor to Széchenyi than a companion or follower. In the West, the large and powerful middle nobility played an important role in the age, which was actively seeking the advancement of the bourgeoisie. Transylvania was a step behind in this as well and here the enlightened highest nobles set the tone. Yet, at the same time, the county delegates in Transylvania were recruited from a much broader base than in Hungary.

The Reform Age was deeply entangled in the language question. Its leaders had distanced themselves from Latin and had rejected German. They identified the use of the Hungarian language with the national aspirations and this raised significant opposition among the national minorities, not any

more against the Austrian-German language, but
against the Hungarian language and the national
aspirations it represented. In addition, the religious
issues also raised their head. Austria was almost
entirely Catholic, while Hungary showed a much
more colorful religious map. The issue of religious
freedom was quite different in Hungary, where
Hungarians following different religions lived
together, than in Transylvania, where the religions
followed ethnic dividing lines. In Transylvania, any-
one speaking up for equal rights for the Greek
Orthodox religion – as many counties had done –
involuntariliy but clearly strengthened the national
pride and national identification of the Transylvanian
Romanians. This, in turn, led to major contradictions, the effects of which did not become manifest
until 1848-1849, and came to a peak after 1918.

The Transylvanian intellectuals were becoming
increasingly better informed. The new models came
from further away, and included western European
Protestantism and the societal and economic changes
it brought. The models also included the English
middle-class, industrial developments and the
French enlightenment and revolution. These intellectuals had made a few study tours to the United
States, and came back with the highest hopes about
the rosy picture of American democracy as applied
to Transylvania. They forgot the circumstances of
America's birth as a nation, and its very different his-
toric-societal origins.

Sándor Bölöni Farkas (1795-1842) resembled
Kőrösi Csoma physically so much that they could
have been taken for twins. He crossed the Atlantic in

1831-1832 and published his *Travel in North America* in 1834. He described his experiences and he was the first one to make available in Hungarian the entire text of the Declaration of Independence and other papers of state and documents of freedom.

Among Hungarians, but particularly in Transylvania, Bölöni's work was the Bible of the intellectual and political elite for many years. Having the work officially condemned added to its popularity. Let us not forget, however, that among the readers we find the Romanian intellectuals who spoke Hungarian, and there were many of these. This book meant liberty for them as well. Needless to say, Bölöni was a friend and associate of Miklós Wesselényi. It was characteristic of the moment that the newly recovering Transylvanian spirit made Vienna see the specter of another Romanian popular uprising. It was a schizophrenic situation. The Court was simultaneously trembling because of these events and was also inciting the Romanians since it was scared even more of Hungarian separatism. Yet – as far as tactics were concerned – the immediate Hungarian aim was no more than an internal structural reorganization of the Habsburg Empire.

Everywhere that timely reforms are forcefully prevented, it is axiomatic that when the changes come anyway, they will be full of unexpected conflicts. Much more threatening to the **Reform Age** was the revision of the serf system as a first step toward complete abolition which, while very complex, was also inevitable. The land reform made antagonists of the nobles and the serfs. The reform illuminated their condition and made it more difficult for the serfs to avail themselves of the centuries-old, routine escape hatches and secret transitions to freedom. When reforms are mandated by the State, one can be certain that the State was going to be the principal beneficiary.

This is very interesting, since those of us who were taught an almost mechanistic development of history and an evolution of human rights from slavery through feudalism to a bourgeois, capitalistic society were amazed to find that the supposedly rigid class society was actually quite flexible. The serf had many opportunities for both individual and family happiness, and had many "special pathways" that were hardly special, and affected very large groups of individuals.

Another matter that was fraught with contradictions and that was very much in the forefront of public concern at this time – somewhat differently in Hungary than in Transylvania – was the issue of the county system. This system simultaneously gave a refuge to the conservative elements of the noble classes and opportunities to the reform party. It could serve both the centralist tendencies of the Court and the Hungarian drive for autonomy. It was increasingly less suitable for the recognition and resolution of minority interests.

Yet another controversy arose from the developments in public education. While increasingly large numbers, including minorities, were provided with middle and higher education, many fewer achieved the opportunities, livelihoods and offices that they had hoped for. Among both the Hungarians and the minorities there was an abundance of intellectuals, but in different proportions. There was a real irony in all this. The educated and fundamentally politically oriented multitude, which was also the victim of discrimination, lacking other employment, became a willing participant in a revolution.

In the meantime, in Pest-Buda, Pozsony, and other centers, law students had a major role in the preparation of the 1848-49 events. Sometimes far from home, these young Romanian, Slovakian, Serb, Croatian, Ruthenian and other university graduates gathered in coffee houses and other societies, established newspapers and prepared to free their own – potential – nation from the icy grip of the Habsburg empire. Many of them saw their adversary not in Vienna, but in Buda, Kolozsvár, and Pozsony. They did not – at least not yet – contemplate a complete separation from Vienna, but rather some internal reforms which would liberate them not so much from Habsburg oppression, but from the much more intimately experienced Hungarian supremacy.

This relative abundance of intellectuals affected the most advanced society in Transylvania, the Saxons as well. Their own particular dilemma was that while they were interested in liberalization because of their bourgeois status and because of their economic interests, their fear of the Hungarians – and more immediately of the official use of the Hungarian language – drove them away from their national interests toward the conservative, centralizing Vienna. At the same time, their greatest concern was the increasing numerical preponderance of

the Romanians, which began to appear in the Saxon
lands as well.

At the beginning of 1846, the national uprising of
the Galician Polish nobility against the Tsarist regime
was drowned in blood by the local peasantry. This
led to two very different interpretations. In Vienna it
meant that this was a good example and a potential
highway to the future; In Buda, among the Hungarian
nobility, it meant that the aspirations of the serfs had
to be supported from above, since otherwise the
Galician example represented a major threat.

The Fight for Freedom,
the Compromise, Dualism

*I*n March 1848, the European revolutionary fever passed though Vienna, Pozsony, and Pest, and rapidly reached Transylvania. Of the twelve Hungarian demands for liberty, it is the twelfth one that rang the bell: "Union with Transylvania". Initially, this was supported by numerous Romanians and Saxons, but public opinion quickly changed. An increasing number in their circle opposed it or would accept the Union only with extensive guarantees of their rights. The Court clearly expected that – with Saxonia as a backstop – it could mobilize the Romanian peasantry and thus surround the rebellious Hungarians. This not only strengthened the Transylvanian Romanians but it might have also produced a strong attraction for the Transcarpathian Romanians to become integrated into the Habsburg Empire. This goal anticipated the present Greater Romania but, of course, strictly within the Monarchy.

There was no secret organization between the ethnic groups – it was only the logic of the situation that was at work. The 1848 Eastern-Central European wildfire spread – after some minor and insignificant manifestations. On May 11-12, 1848, the Slovakians presented their principal national demands at Liptószentmiklós. The Serbs followed on May 13-15 at Karlóca, and the Romanians at their national assembly in Balázsfalva, on May 15-17. This latter city was, at this time already an important center for Romanian religious and educational affairs, and the selection of this site was evidence for the major role played by the intellectuals.

On the eve of the last meeting, on May 14, a local professor of philosophy, Simion Barnutiu, gave a speech in the Balázsfalva cathedral. "This speech is the basic text for the Romanian national idea and the most significant expression of Romanian national consciousness since the Supplex. It emphasizes the right of the Romanians for self determination and states that every morsel cast to them from the table of Hungarian liberty is poisoned." (Samu Benkő.)

Just like the Transylvanian Hungarians, the Romanian intellectual elite looked more and more toward the Western world. There was a discussion at Balázsfalva about the Western European trends toward national states, which may have served as a model for the smaller states. Here we had the first mention of the later so popular concept of an "Eastern European Switzerland". The obvious Panslavism warned the non Slavs to get together. It did not happen here, but soon there was talk about a Danubian Confederation, with a forceful reversal of ethnic mingling and a massive exchange of populations. Is there anything new under the sun? This could well be a question raised by an observer today.

It comes as no surprise that all Transylvania was reaching for arms. Even though the ethnic groups did this in good faith and for their own protection, it was clearly the first step toward civil war. All it needed was a tiny spark, anywhere and for any real or imaginary injury.

In Hungary, the freeing of the serfs took place, although not without some injuries and some conflicts. How about Transylvania? Here the process was impeded by the different local civil laws. If, however, the Union was going to assure equal laws everywhere, what was the problem? Unfortunately the legal and practical implementation of the Union was not a simple matter. It required multiple approvals in the Vienna-Pest-Transylvania triangle. The differing internal systems did not allow the mechanical extension of the Hungarian legal system. The other parties, and particularly the Romanian serfs, suspected that these were delaying tactics, tricks and sabotage on the part of the Hungarian nobility. This in spite of the fact that the last Transylvanian Diet, called without the approval of the Emperor, already freed 160,000 families at the end of March, and that most of these were Romanian. This is the stumbling block in every major change of system: the changes occasioned forcefully by the revolutionary enthusiasm stand on legally shaky ground and the legal process is necessarily slow. There is a period in all such changes when the old system is no longer functional, and the new system is not yet in place. A fact unfortunately remains a fact: in this confusion, the first fatal shots were fired by Székely border guards in a police action, with Romanian peasants caught in the middle, illegally using grazing land.

The Transylvanian Romanians were unsure about the serf problem, but this is not all. The revolution extended to their natural allies, the Romanians in the Regate. This was suppressed by Turkish-Russian cooperation. Bucharest was occupied. They wanted to get rid of their other potential ally, the Serbs. The reason being the strong influence the Serb Orthodox Church had on the Romanian Orthodox Church. There were thus obvious factors that should have promoted a consideration of Romanian-Hungarian cooperation.

When the fall of 1848 began, the Croatian troops of Jelačić started their sneak attack against the Hungarian capital from the south and, in the east, Transylvania came to a boil. The establishment of the first army of the responsible Hungarian government required conscription. Even though shortly rescinded, this triggered a protest – even among some Hungarians – which then led to a new Balázsfalva assembly and encampment, this time of several weeks' duration. There was a demand that the very shaky, but established union be dissolved. It also led to the situation where the Austrian troops stationed in Transylvania could very soon count on large numbers of auxiliaries in the form of substantial Romanian rebel troops.

It got worse. The Kossuth people wishing to mobilize the Székelys for participation in the civil war gathered about 60 thousand armed Székelys in Agyagfalva on October 16, 1848. The fact that here the emphasis was placed on Hungarian affairs rather than on the revolution, that the goals and agenda were not sufficiently clarified, and that some of the Székely leaders starting from Agyagfalva were more interested in creating confusion than in anything else, were the causes that made the Transylvanian tragedy of the fall of 1848 resemble an avalanche. The people of Balázsfalva and Agyagfalva and many other Transylvanian communities, groups and associations, stood face to face. It was a miracle that the Austrian military leaders, indecisive and misunderstanding the local situation, could not take greater advantage of this conflict.

The Hungarian Diet and government – engaged in a life and death struggle – were unable to, or delayed in, issuing ordinances that could have calmed and pacified the nationalities. Many of these were of the opinion anyway, that the attack of Jelačić is going to be victorious, and that they may just as well stand on the winning side. This opinion was shared by the Saxons, who were becoming increasingly aware of their German blood ties.

In this difficult situation – and as we have seen, without adequate thought – the Hungarian government did not limit its mobilization to the militarily experienced Székelys. A national guard was being organized throughout Transylvania, but the Hungarians were reluctant to attack. They could expect nothing good from a general civil war. After the Balázsfalva and Agyagfalva assemblies, there were already wide-spread clashes and retributions that caused considerable damage to both sides. All in vain. The Austrian General Puchner, the military commander of Transylvania, ordered his troops and their Romanian auxiliaries to disarm the Hungarian national troops. This did not take place without much bloodshed and much damage and destruction to civilian and public property.

The upsurge of long suppressed hatreds and the murderous heat of the moment made the map of Transylvania into a bloody mosaic. In October and November of 1848, clashes here, battles there and in some places even massacres decorated the map. It appeared that this region was lost. Finally, only Háromszék held out, but this made it impossible for Vienna to take the central Hungarian forces into a pincer movement. In many areas the anti-Hungarian cooperation began to yield rewards and a new, essentially Romanian administration was being established.

At this time it was no longer the post-revolutionary government of the steadfast and sober Lajos Batthyány which was in charge "over there". It was the much more radical Committee of National Defense which now governed the country forced into a national fight for freedom. The center of gravity of the events was shifting toward the east. The capital on the Danube was first threatened and then lost and the new capital was moved to Debrecen. The armament factory of Pest was moved to Nagyvárad. Kossuth appointed a new commander in chief for Transylvania. He was the Polish József Bem (1794-1850), whose name we consistently spell in the Hungarian way. Considering the forces and means at his disposal, he fought a very successful winter campaign and reconquered almost all of Transylvania. From whom? Primarily from the armies of the Austrian General Puchner who also had a new commander-in-chief. The family had removed the incompetent Ferdinand V (1835-1848) and replaced him with his young nephew, Francis Joseph (1848-1916).

It would take too long to follow Bem's Transylvania campaign in detail, during which this romantic and daring revolutionary and military commander made several, almost desperate attempts on his own authority to win over the nationalities. It must be mentioned, however, that the Russian intervention into the Hungarian civil war began here and now. On Puchner's plea for help – he claimed that the Romanians were responsible for this – a 3,000 member Tsarist army entered Transylvania across the Southern Carpathians in February 1849. Bem chased them and their Austrian hosts back to the Havasalföld. Tsar Nicholas I now, at the beginning of May, decided to save the House of Habsburg, and in the middle of June sent a 200,000 men Russian deluge from the north, across the Dukla Pass into Hungary. All the rest was just a question of time.

In the meantime, the "Olmütz Constitution" of Francis Joseph declared that Transylvania was an independent province. This was countered by the Debrecen Declaration which deposed the House of Habsburg. A desperate measure which scared many previous supporters away from the civil war which was considered to be a constitutional battle when viewed from the Hungarian perspective. The declaration was issued jointly in the names of Hungary and Transylvania as a matter of course.

After Bem's triumphs, Transylvania was almost completely in Hungarian hands during the spring and summer of 1849. What was then the situation? Would magnanimity or Draconian severity triumph?

Would the earlier collaboration be overlooked or revenged? Bem covered the past deeds with an amnesty, but the future was going to be judged by the court-martial set up by Kossuth's local governors. Morality apart, this was not a wise thing to do, even if there had been something to avenge. Burning the great center of learning, Nagyvárad, together with its library, for example, took many lives to make its point. The rapid deterioration of the military situation made all of these issues moot, including a last minute attempt at Hungarian-Romanian conciliation.

The capitulation at Világos on August 13, 1849 did not affect Bem's troops, but the consequences were entirely beyond their control. The time came when it was impossible to tell the difference between the punishment that the deliriously victorious Vienna meted out to the Hungarians and the benefits they bestowed on the other nationalities in Hungary. It was certain that already early in September the Austrian commander-in-chief issued an order for the dismissal of the Romanian auxiliary troops. The loyal Saxons got their unpleasant surprises a little later. The Saxon lands were dismembered and their autonomy was revoked.

As it happens not infrequently, regardless of what the reactionary forces may do for their own gratification after the victorious termination of a civil war, many results and consequences of the civil war remain. There could be no question of the re-establishment of serfdom or of a complete reconstruction of the old cast system of society. In a paradoxical way, some of the things that were done against the

central Austrian power, turned out to be to its benefit. The modernizations promoting the development
of a bourgeoisie, which was a vital interest of the
House of Habsburg, was much easier to implement
– even forcefully – at this time. The evolutionary
processes, that begun under Maria Theresa and
Joseph II, and were sustained under the Reform Age
came to their inevitable fruition at this time. There
was an opportunity to introduce and implement
"from above" without there being an opportunity to
resist "from below". Needless to say, this was a
painful process, which took place under foreign
officials and executors, under a tight military occupation.

The Bach Era, universally condemned in Hungary,
actually had both good and bad features. The new
administration, legal system, law enforcement and
their executive apparatus were foreign, but although
oppressive, they granted a number of advantages in
the non-political arena. Public safety was much
improved and, more importantly, numerous economic innovations were introduced and the bases
for economic development were stabilized. Yet, this
was the period when in our region, and with a fatal
intensity, there appeared a permanent opposition to
all governments and to the legal system of all administrations. All this, of course, was disguised as an
absolutely patriotic endeavor. This kind of "civil
disobedience" is well known from Northern Ireland
to the Basque country, but is fortunately unknown
in most of Western Europe.

The entire Hungarian political situation – which
was supposed to enlighten and instruct the frigh-

tened and confused Transylvanian Hungarians – was now increasingly under the influence of Ferenc Deák (1803-1876). Known as the "Sage of the Fatherland", he was patient, he opposed the Debrecen Declaration deposing the Habsburg dynasty, and he was willing to wait until a way was found toward a compromise. Until then, he favored passive civil resistance and a prudent retrenchment.

The Deák inspired wisdom and passivity in "high politics" was reduced at the "popular" level to the avoidance of taxation, of duties and of income tax, and even to the escape from military service, by any means ingenuity could devise. This was not only considered to be not shameful, but it was a glorious thing to do. The people, by the Grace of God, had learned during the centuries of serfdom, how to mislead its masters, to avoid the foreign armies exacting tribute, to hide itself and its goods. It was now using this accumulated wisdom against the detested Bach officials and against the Austrian soldiers quartered on them. Unfortunately, they maintained this mentality even when they became the citizens of their own national state. They considered it a virtue – and do so even today – if they could take advantage of a to them "foreign" administration.

The country was full of mutterings rather than with useful activity, and there were many Hungarian underground, hole and corner groups. The most important anti-Austrian organization, after 1849, took place in Transylvania. It was naive and nurtured the image of an ambitious new beginning. Its leader was a Colonel József Makk, who lived in Bucharest and who was going to arm the Székely rebels with weapons obtained from Moldavia. The anticipated, new European wave of revolutions on which they pinned their hopes did not materialize. The Viennese spies were watchful and the conspirators were careless. The movement, that actually reached as far as Vienna, collapsed after its leaders were arrested. Even though the institution of serfdom was legally abolished in Transylvania during the summer of 1848, by the declaration of the Diet of that year, and a law was enacted about universal taxation, the effective freeing of the serfs was made very difficult by the complicated ownership and legal conditions, the numerous tacit individual arrangements, based on common law, and the virtual impossibility of assessing the value of the socage, for the loss of which the landowners were supposed to receive compensation. Much bad feeling was generated by a discussion about the disposition of the jointly and freely used forests – which were considered to be inexhaustible.

"Down below", this affected the Romanians most of all. They were numerically the largest group that felt itself to be despoiled during their serfdom and who were most dependent on their pastoral privileges and on the free use of the forests. The landowner group was equally impoverished, since it was paid only the already minimal compensation. The payments were made in devalued Treasury bonds, and the compensation was further reduced by the War Tax imposed by Vienna at the time of the Crimean War. With the exception of the officials and the men in the repressive organizations – mostly Austrians,

Czechs and Moravians – almost everybody considered himself a looser.

While the Hungarians are fond of mentioning the key strategic role of the Carpathian basin in Central Europe, we must not forget the geopolitical power held by whoever controlled the historically so drafty passage between the Carpathians and the Black Sea, including the estuary of the Danube. This area was both a bridge and a divider between the northern Slavs and the southern Slavs. At the foot of the Alps a strong German wedge was driven between these two groups and in the Carpathian basin a Hungarian wedge was inserted at the time of the Conquest. To the east of the Carpathians the Romanians settled who came north from the mid-Balkans and from Macedonia, speaking a Neo-Latin, much more Thracian than Dacian, and strongly intermingled in their new home with Cumanians, Pechenegs, Slavs and others. They left behind themselves small groups at the Albanian – Macedonian – Greek borderland, in Salonika and in the Istrian Peninsula. These groups, while decreasing steadily, are still recognizable today by the language they speak. The strongest, north-eastern group of the Romanians slowly and against massive opposition, reached an area along the lower Danube and reached a status just short of forming a nation. This had been mentioned above, in passing.

In 1853, Tsarist Russian troops marched along the foothills of the Carpathians, this time against the Turks. This led to the above mentioned Crimean War and to a crushing Russian defeat. Austria, forgetting its indebtedness to Nicholas I, occupied the Moldavian and Havasalföld Romanian principalities for several years. Finally, and in order to maintain the balance of power among the distant major European powers, Turkey irretrievably lost control over this area, but neither Russia nor Austria could acquire it. Moldavia and the Havasalföld, recently enlarged, first became independent and then formed a personal union in 1859. The ruling prince, Alexandru Ioan Cuza (1820-1873) now got in touch with the 1849 Hungarian emigrés. In exchange for future assistance, he asked for military support for himself to conquer all of Bessarabia, and he naturally also asked for an expansion of the rights of the Transylvanian Romanians. Even the possibility of a triple Romanian-Serb-Hungarian confederation was raised, which in the dreams of Kossuth became the Romanian-Serb-Croatian-Hungarian Danubian Confederation. All this was put on hold by the general European realignments. Austria lost both territory and power in Italy and in the Prussian War but this could be used against her only later. Even then the beneficiaries were Deák and his followers and not the Kossuth group.

The icy grip of the Bach Era began to thaw. There was an inevitable, cautious liberalization from above with a partial re-establishment of Parliament. It was a bitter lesson for the Hungarians that this narrowly defined census-based election resulted in a Romanian majority in the Transylvanian Diet. "The 1863 summer elections – during which the government is alleged to have spent 800 thousand Forints to influence approximately 70-89,000 voters – 49 Romanian, 44 Hungarian and 33 Saxon candidates received a mandate. The Hungarian liberal camp got the mandates in all of the Székely *széks* and in all the Hungarian cities, but in the counties which were considered to be the ancient, fundamental units of political life, they suffered a disastrous defeat. Of the 38 county representatives only 2 were Hungarians. The king nominated 11 'men of substance', or officials, from each nationality, assigning to them a balancing function which in other countries was performed by an Upper House. In the final count there were 60 (later 59) Romanian, 56 Hungarian and 44 Saxon representatives with a seat in the Diet." (Zoltán Szász.)

Opting for absentee obstruction, only three Hungarian representatives showed up. This effectively neutralized the organization about which the above writer said: "This was the first – and also the last – Transylvanian Diet in which the Romanians were present as a national block and even represented a majority." – And something else. While the legitimacy of this Parliament was debatable and its effectiveness in view of the Hungarian boycott was limited, it was this organization which made the three Transylvanian languages, Romanian, Hungarian and German, of equal legal standing.

Let us examine the demographic basis of the 1863 election results. We may get the best lead from the religious statistics. In 1850, in Transylvania proper, without the Partium, the numbers were as follows: Greek Orthodox 32.3%, Greek Catholic 29.2% (together 61.51%), Reformed 13.6%, Roman Catholic 11.4%, Evangelical 10.5%, Unitarian 2.4 %, and Jewish 0.6%.

It must be noted that the religious affiliations change little until 1910 or until the beginning of

World War I. The major change was the decrease of the Greek Orthodox to 29.6%, while the number of Jews increased to 2.4%, due to increased immigration during the second half of the last century, and to the large number of children in their families. Thus, the fraction of the almost exclusively Romanian Greek Orthodox decreased and the number of children became a factor with the Jews and not with them. Contrary to popular belief, in the time span under discussion, namely 1851 to 1857, the increase in Transylvanian Lutherans was practically zero (0.12%). The increase of the other two Protestant denominations was 0.7% and the same number applies to the Greek Orthodox. The increase in Roman Catholics was 0.9% and in Greek Catholics it was 0.57%. It is interesting that the one and two children families were most prominent among the Saxons and the Svabians in the Banate, the former of whom were Lutheran and the latter Roman Catholic. Among the peculiarly local Unitarians the birth rate was so low that it practically amounted to a denominational suicide.

Two additional set of data. The first one comes already from the turn of the century, and states that while the total percentage of the Roman Catholics was 13.3%, they represented 25.9% of the urban population. Among the Reformed, the total was 14.7% while the urban percentage was 23.4%. Among the Lutherans these numbers were 9% versus 16.1%. Among the Jews 2.1% versus 6.3%. The situation was reversed among the Greek Catholics whose percentage of the population was 28%, while they represented only 11.6% of the urban population. Among the Greek Orthodox, these numbers were 30.3% versus 15%. Thus, the majority of the latter two groups was rural and they represented only a small percentage of the urban population. This had to give rise to substantial speculation both for the present time, and also for the foreseeable future.

Returning to the mid-century, let us examine the distribution on the basis of native language. In Transylvania proper, in 1850, 58.3% were Romanians, 26.1% Hungarians, 10.3% Germans, 4% Gypsies, 0.6% Yiddish, 0.4% Armenians, and all others 0.2%. Those who assume that there was a Hungarization during the following half century, naturally at the expense of the Romanians, must be reminded that in 1900, those who claimed to have Hungarian as their mother tongue increased by 6.7% to 32.8%, while the Romanian speakers decreased by 1.75 to 56.9%. The increase in Hungarian speakers must be attributed to the fact that in 1850 there were 4% who claimed to have the Gypsy language as their mother tongue. In 1900 this category no longer appeared in the list. It can be assumed that at this time the entire Gypsy ethnic group was included among the Hungarian speakers.

One additional item. According to one estimate, at the turn of the century Bucharest had 200,000 Hungarian inhabitants (ethnic?, or Hungarian speaking?). At the same time there were very many emigrants to America, but also to Germany. This drained primarily the Székelyföld. It seemed to prove the frequently made allegation that the group making up the majority of the participants in the "classic" emigration were not necessarily those who came from the most miserable circumstances. Rather, they came from groups that had already achieved a certain level of prosperity, but who were stuck there and who because of their family and national traditions wanted more and better things. It was not the multitude of solo flute playing, mountain shepherds who struck out toward the New World, but the Jack-of-all-trades, skilled Székelys who made up the bulk of the emigrants.

When forging the Compromise of 1867, one of the Hungarian demands was the re-establishment of the 1848 union. But, as we can recall, the union did not have the enthusiastic endorsement of the two principal Transylvanian nationalities, the Romanians and the Saxons, and therefore the new Hungarian state, now an "integral partner" in the Austro-Hungarian Monarchy, decided to proceed cautiously. Thus, Transylvania was not immediately integrated into the motherland.

On the other hand, already in 1868 a Nationality Act was passed which was extremely progressive by the standards of the time, and which was much more meaningful at the periphery of the country than in its central parts. This act could serve as a model even today, since it accepted the use of the mother tongue in both official and other applications, permitted separate schooling and the establishment of separate national organizations in each "civilian society". It also granted collective rights, and not just individual ones. It can justly serve as a basis for reference. As far as its implementation was concerned, the picture is less attractive.

In the case of such legislation, it is customary that initially there is a strong "customer resistance" which weakens over time. Here the reverse occurred. While the Compromise was a success in the economic sphere, the Hungarians of the Monarchy vigorously pursued what they considered to be the most precious part of their existence, namely, Hungarization and the acceptance of Hungarian supremacy, both of which they considered to be their lawful aspirations. The hopes and aspirations generated by the favorable Nationality Act of 1868 decreased rather than increased with time, learning the Hungarian language became compulsory in all schools, and the nationality schools could no longer accept foreign contributions. Since the counties were usually the bastions of conservatism, the extension of the county system to Transylvania – to the detriment of the Székely and Saxon legal traditions – was a regressive development.

We must add one thing about the 1868 Nationality Act, linked to the names of Ferenc Deák and József Eötvös (1813-1871). This legal document, significant even by general European standards, was based on the concept of the French nationality-state and emphasized in its introduction that "according to the fundamental principles of the Constitution, and in a political context, all citizens of the country together constitute a single nation, an indivisible, unified, Hungarian nation, of which every citizen of the country, regardless of national affiliation, is an equal member, having the same legal rights."

What is wrong with it? It contains the terms "political context" and "equal rights"... Yet, the passage was condemned in the strongest terms by the authors of a Romanian memorandum in 1892, who wrote, "In other words, every human being living in Hungary, be they Romanian, German, Slavic, etc., belong to a single nation, the Hungarian. It goes without saying that we view this introduction as an overt assault against our national existence and against the national existence of our other non-Hungarian fellow citizens." This was the official position of the Romanians from 1868 until 1918, when the die turned in precisely the opposite direction. This is in effect to this day and the Hungarians and Székelys in Transylvania, must (should) declare and consider themselves as Hungarian speaking Romanians and members of the Romanian national state.

The electoral system of 1848, while expanded on the basis of property, education, and other criteria, was still quite restrictive and not uniformly applied. In the more backward Transylvania, amendments were necessary. In spite of this, at the beginning of the 1880s only a quarter of the Transylvanian Saxons, a fifth of the Hungarians, and barely a tenth of the Romanians had the vote. This was not the sole determinant factor. Because of their large numbers, the Romanians had a majority in some electoral districts. It was a different issue that – due to certain circumstances discussed below – it happens that these districts, with a Romanian majority, provided the safest seats for the government, even though the government's nationality policy hardly deserved this.

The forty years following the Compromise were not the golden age in everything, not even economically, even though east of the Lajta the advances were dynamic. The greatest stimulus for this upswing was the capital pouring into this area. It did not stop at a new water barrier, the Danube, or at Budapest, which was increasingly openly competing with Vienna. Yet the railroad initially only extended as far as Temesvár, Arad, and Nagyvárad. Its further extension was slow, partly because of the increasingly difficult geographic conditions. The situation was similar in the area of road building. The large unified customs area of the Monarchy had much to offer, but the more backward peripheral areas could take only limited advantage of this for their own advancement.

For Transylvania, the most important issue was the trade with Romania – we must finally admit this. Export and import were the keys, but the Monarchy got embroiled in such a customs battle in the east that these very dynamic relationships were severely curtailed. There is no chapter in the picture book of Hungarian economic and industrial development that was not enriched by spectacular Transylvanian contributions. The strikingly executed art and the beautiful creations in wrought iron document not only past developments and virtues, but are also eloquent witnesses of to human diligence, inventiveness, care, and abundance of talent.

While the basis for the struggle were the Hungarian – and Romanian and Saxon – national identity issues, the ideological and political factors also carried considerable weight. When, with the 1868 Compromise the Hungarian search for a national identity achieved its objectives and gained momentum, this momentum was obtained simultaneously by various nationalities and shifted the center of gravity of the dualistic Monarchy. Let's put it this way. In the struggle for political and economic strong points, the latter became the more important ones. The Hungarian Cultural Association of Transylvania (EMKE), as its name clearly indicates, was not exactly established for this purpose, but it quickly recognized the trend, albeit perhaps not the full weight of the trend. It originally started with nationalistic and educational aims, but rapidly shifted toward the establishment and protection of commercial enterprises. The Transylvanian Economic Association (EGE), established in 1844, was active in the same area.

The Saxon fear of the oppressive Dual Monarchy was much relieved when it became apparent that their age-old, characteristic economic activity and influence would not be affected. In fact the economic revival favored those who already had an earlier start. It is true that among the Saxons a new political orientation began which turned away from the Austrians and pointed toward a "Greater Germany". At this time and in contrast to the Hitler era, the Saxons received little encouragement from this direction. For the Wilhelmine-Bismarckian Germany good relations with Austria and Hungary were much more important than a possible separatist tendency among the now 200 thousand strong Saxons.

While the Saxons were becoming increasingly resigned to the union, the Romanians were becoming increasingly hostile. They realized that if Transylvania were to become autonomous, their numerical superiority would become decisive. Their interests were not identical everywhere. The Romanians living outside Transylvania in Hungary tried to get ahead in that country. The Transylvanian Romanians were more "fundamentalists", and selected passivity as one of the options in the all-or-nothing game of political resistance. This tactic is difficult to justify fully, and goes a long way to explain why the government had such an easy time of it in the primarily Romanian electoral districts. At this time, the number of those who demanded an autonomous Transylvania or who turned toward the extra-Transylvanian Romanians was negligible. The majority of the Romanians had little understanding for this policy. They voted indifferently for whoever seemed to represent a power base, or from whom they hoped to gain some advantages, a decrease in harassment, a road, a small bridge, etc. This was offered most effectively by the existing government. It is noteworthy that when in 1881 a unified Romanian National Party was established, a certain Partenie Cosma was elected president. He was a lawyer, employed by a large bank. The importance of banks as a source of capital was increasing in the peripheral areas as well.

What was happening in the meantime in the area beyond the Carpathians? Moldavia and the Havas-alföld increasingly fused into a personal union and formed a principality under the leadership of Cuza.

Since 1861 it was called Romania, and very soon Bucharest became the capital of the principality. Cuza's gentrifying, liberal "forward-looking" laws produced a violent reaction. In 1866 he was expelled and the still evolving but inchoate country looked abroad for a new ruler. This was not entirely strange and there were many historic precedents. It was strange, however, that while the Neo-Latin speaking Romanians were oriented toward Paris and were linked in their higher ideals – other than to antiquity – to the French cultural circles, the new ruler was a Prussian Hohenzollern.

The beginnings of Charles I (1866 or rather 1881-1914) were fortunate. When in 1877-78, the Russian Tsar again tried to limit the Turkish area of influence, the Romanian troops commanded by him participated successfully in the Russia campaign. This then irrevocably eliminated any danger that the age-old and detrimental Turkish influence might have held for the fledgling Romania. The fact that at this precise moment some Hungarian circles developed a Russophobe and Turkophile attitude distorted the picture and did little to promote Hungarian-Romanian relationships. Apparently the memories of 1849 were more vivid than those of the much earlier Turkish occupation. This went to the point where a small volunteer group was being formed which wished to fight on the side of the Turks in this conflict. When a Romanian counter-force was being developed, the Hungarian government quickly stepped in.

In the Peace of San Stefano, the declining Turkish sultanate was forced to recognize the independence of Romania, which changed its form of government in 1881. *Nota bene,* the new Romanian kingdom, under the same Charles I, proved to be just as ungrateful toward Russia as Austria had been. Having gotten rid of the Turkish influence, it very soon did the same with Russia, by turning to Vienna and Berlin and by forming a secret alliance with these countries. This turn of events moderated Bucharest's attempts to incorporate Transylvania. Initially such an attempt was foremost among the plans of the new kingdom, and was based on the often stated Daco-Roman Continuity hypothesis. The moderation was only partial and temporary. The economic driving force of the Compromise was still unbroken and may even have reached its peak, but the euphoria was gone. Furthermore, it was 1896 and the approaching millennium of the original conquest created an enthusiasm in Hungarian public opinion that made it impossible politically to handle even the moderate requests of the nationalities with understanding. One can imagine the reaction of the Orthodox Romanians to the ordinance that made Hungarian mandatory in religious instruction. It was of no consequence that ordinances, like the one just mentioned, or the one forbidding the multilingual posting of the name of a community, were never really enforced. This did little to mitigate the insult. It should have been a warning when Serb and Slovak attorneys were retained for the defense in a trial of the distributors of a Romanian memorandum about minority rights of which, initially, neither the Vienna Court nor the Hungarian government took official notice. The prosecution was started, after considerable hesitation, in Kolozsvár in 1882. The choice of attorneys showed a definite and demonstrative cooperation.

Sober Romanian observers noticed an old trap: the divisiveness within their ranks and the excessive impatience were less harmful to the cause of the Romanians than the benefits they gained from the fundamentalism of the Hungarian power elite which had become their unwitting ally. There was much they could refer to when they took the injuries of the minorities from the Hungarian to the European stage. The above mentioned ordinance was promptly translated into half a dozen leading European languages. It was at this time – and unfortunately not entirely without foundation – that a picture was painted of the Hungarians for the benefit of the European community which would have been more accurate for a conquering-adventuring Scythian robber band than for the citizens of a country which since 1868 had made every effort, economically and politically, to model itself on the rest of Western Europe. The attempts of the Czech Tomas Masaryk (1850-1937) and of the Romanian Ion Brătianu (1867-1927) to use this distorted caricature of the Hungarians in their efforts to dismember the Monarchy received an irresponsible assist from a very odd individual, the well-known British historian, Seton-Watson, known under his pen name as Scotus Viator. His increasingly prejudiced works clearly influenced the misinformed decision makers of the desperately unfair peace treaties at the end of World War I.

After the turn of the century, Hungarian politics became increasingly involved in prestige fights rather than rational controversies and these for all practical purposes rendered the Dual Monarchy impotent. We once again see the collusion between the Court and the nationalities in the expansion of the franchise by imperial fiat rather than by legitimate parliamentary action. Even greater weight was given to this situation by the tragic death at Mayerling of Crown Prince Rudolph. Rudolph liked the Hungarians and, had he lived, might have become a more progressive ruler than Joseph II. He particularly liked Transylvania. One of his faithful friends was the strange Transylvanian magnate, Count Samu Teleki, the hero of a celebrated African expedition. Rudolph frequently hunted on Teleki's Sáromberk estate. The sentiments and views of the new Crown Prince, Francis Ferdinand, were diametrically opposed to those of Rudolph, who wrote liberal articles under a pen name. Francis Ferdinand wanted to rely on the nationalities to create a strong counterbalance against the Hungarians. Not knowing how long Francis Joseph would continue to live, he instigated numerous cabals, feeding the hopes of his initiates. It is one of history's ironies that it was a Serb nationalist who shot him down in Sarajevo in 1914.

The most influential Hungarian politician during the decade and a half, following the turn of the century, was the deeply conservative but yet pragmatic István Tisza (1861-1918), a highly manipulative party leader and twice prime minister. The center of gravity of political infighting was now located in

Parliament, as it was in most modern states. In this arena the representatives of the nationalities were necessarily a small minority, entirely at the mercy of the benevolence or caprice of the majority nationality. With increasingly destructive obstructionist maneuvers, the opposition paralyzed and re-paralyzed the life of the Parliament. Tisza, reviled by many, used every trick, ruse and force to maintain the country's ability to function. He even had enough energy left to attempt a reconciliation with the Romanians, if necessary, at the price of suppressing the Transylvanian Hungarian representatives. He realized that to achieve some compromise solution, the support of Bucharest, representing all the Romanians, was more important than the support of the Transylvanian politicians who had become inflexible in their self-serving local interests. His offer was necessarily limited by the Hungarian political situation and by his own way of thinking. This offer was also in opposition to the one made by Francis Ferdinand, who at this time lacked any authority for so doing. According to the nationalities, if they had to live under a monarchy, this had to be multipolar rather than the dualistic monarchy that in the past had granted the Hungarians too much authority.

Very shortly all of this became tragically meaningless by the obligation to adhere to the German goals and by an Austria filled with new imperial ambitions that not only participated in the Balkan punitive campaign – soon to become expanded into World War I – but actually initiated it by the coarse and insulting ultimatum to Serbia, which in fact was a co-conspirator in the Sarajevo outrage. Only a few more days, and the troops hoping to return home "by the time the leaves fall", marched off toward the grave of the Dual Austro-Hungarian Monarchy. Much more is buried in that grave than the frequently condemned, but later even more frequently missed governmental system of Central Europe.

Downfall and Punishment

*W*hen in July 1914 the Monarchy mobilized, hundreds of thousands of men of military age were called up, regardless of their ethnic origin. The bellicose enthusiasm of the Hungarians was without parallel in the Empire. The best informed person, István Tisza, was well aware of their military unpreparedness and soberly assessing the strength of the enemy opposed the war – needles to say, unsuccessfully. He was also concerned about Transylvania, fearing a Romanian invasion. There was no one who could foresee or sense that the war, about to begin, would bring nothing but disaster, quite independently of Transylvania, to the principal ethnic group in the Carpathian basin, the Hungarians. Should the war be victorious, the only beneficiaries would be Austria and Germany. If it's lost? Nobody was prepared to assume Hungary's burden.

Transylvania was once again the apple of Eris. The Romanian Kingdom was technically in a triple alliance with Austria and Germany, but Russia had promised it Transylvania – it did not belong to Russia – and even a part of Bukovina, if Romania were to form an alliance with Russia or even if it only were to remain neutral. This was one of the reasons why István Tisza was so reluctant to enter the war. He saw this ploy very clearly, even though public opinion did not. It was this fact – and also some rather crude pressure from Germany – that forced him to make some concessions to Romania. These were insufficient, however, to satisfy the Transylvanian Romanians or Bucharest. What it did accomplish was to enrage the Hungarian fundamentalists.

As long as the war appeared to go well for the German and Austro-Hungarian forces, the king of Romania held back and carefully preserved his armed forces so much desired by both sides. When the fortunes of war began to turn, he made a secret pact with the Entente Powers, according to which the West recognized his right to Transylvania.

The previous paragraph was written intentionally with complete objectivity. Whoever believes to detect any irony in it is mistaken. The young Romanian state, which carried no responsibility for the outbreak of World War I, decided and acted in the most rational fashion and in the best interest of the Romanian national and ethnic goals. It accepted and even actively sought whatever was most advantageous for it. What nation or country would do otherwise?

In keeping with the above, Romania declared war on the Monarchy, and on August 27, 1916 attacked Transylvania with an army of almost 500,000 men. Since it was opposed only by a few border guard gendarmes – where was the Monarchy's information service? – considerable territorial gains were made by the Romanians within a few weeks. It is noteworthy that the Romanian population of the occupied parts of Transylvania was quite reserved. This came as a surprise to both Bucharest and Vienna-Budapest. Yet this was hardly a sign of their attachment to the Habsburg Empire or to the Hungarians, nor was it a lack of national feeling. It was due more to the fact that they doubted the success of the campaign. Behold! The rapidly transferred Austro-Hungarian and German troops counter-attacked and by early fall pushed the attackers back beyond the Carpathians. It was the result of this victory – Pyrrhic though it may have proved in the future – that Turkey and Bulgaria joined the Vienna-Berlin axis. This prevented any renewal of Romanian attacks against Transylvania for the time being. "After the expulsion of the enemy, spectacular gestures were made to please and calm the Hungarian and Saxon populations. At the beginning of November 1916, the Crown Prince and the King of Bavaria visited the area and during the following fall the Emperor of Germany paid a ceremonial visit to Transylvania. Official and social assistance programs were initiated. At the same time the civil, but particularly the military authorities, initiated inhuman punitive measures against the Romanians – presumably to cover up their guilty feelings for having left Transylvania defenseless. Internments, arrests and indictments followed in rapid succession, even though several hundred thousand Romanians were still fighting bravely under the flags of the Monarchy. During the fall of 1917, the Minister of the Interior admitted to 825 internments, while the Romanians knew of more than one thousand. When the Tisza government was dismissed in the middle of 1917, the new

Minister of Religion and Education, Count Albert Apponyi, began to establish a so-called cultural zone along the borders facing Romania, where public schools were to replace all the religious schools and only the 15-18 most famous educational institutions would remain in the hands of the Romanian Orthodox Church. According to his plans, 1,600 new state schools and kindergartens would be established within 4-5 years. A permanent government inspector-supervisor was appointed for each of the Romanian teacher colleges. In June 1918 all state support was withdrawn in this zone from the 477 teachers employed in the 311 Romanian parochial schools. The restructuring of the schools in the border zone was brought to a sudden end by the events of the fall of 1918." (Zoltán Szász.)

During this time, and in spite of some regional successes, the war machinery of the Central Powers increasingly creaked and cracked, casting the shadow of the final collapse. Yet, on the other side, Russia was also defeated and eliminated from the war and Romania was forced to acknowledge a military defeat. At the peace of May 1918 it had to relinquish Dobrudja to Bulgaria, which at this time was still fighting on the side of the Central Powers. It had to make some border concessions to Hungary as well. But then the effects of the 1918 military collapse, the ensuing revolutionary period and the destruction of the central administration on the Romanian political movements in Transylvania and on the events taking place in this area, need not be related in detail since every event was immediately superseded by the onrushing developments. Suffice it to say that the attempts to promptly repatriate the almost half million Romanian soldiers serving in the disintegrating forces of the Monarchy failed, and the expected assumption of power that this repatriation was supposed to accomplish did not take place.

In compensation and after some initial hesitation, the U.S.A., or rather its "Great Peacemaker" President Wilson, decided that a unified Romania, including Transylvania, shall be established. This plan was also – and shamefully – supported by Germany on condition that it may bring home the still armed and battle-ready Mackensen army from southeastern Romania, where it could have easily become a hostage in Romanian hands. The Károlyi government in Budapest, the product of a middle-class revolution and drifting aimlessly, made a very liberal attempt to consolidate Transylvania with political and legal concessions, announced in Arad by Oszkár Jászi, which went far beyond any previous concessions. It was far too late. 1918 was not even over yet when two parallel events pre-empted any future action. Even though it held only promises and had no legal mandate, the Romanian Royal Army invaded and rapidly occupied Transylvania in November-December. It could do this easily, there was no resistance. (In the northwest, a somewhat earlier Czech invasion was averted by Hungarian units.) On December 1-2, at Gyulafehérvár, a Romanian Diet-Popular Assembly took place which has ever since been considered a milestone in Romanian history. *Nota bene:* This fateful Romanian historic event was strongly supported by the still extant Hungarian administration, and its participants were transported to the meeting by special trains operated by the Hungarian National Railways. It is this Diet which proclaimed Transylvania's union with Romania. There were some conditions which were met and which must be mentioned, since lately they seem to have been forgotten.

The leaders of the Romanian multitude assembled at Gyulafehérvár, who drafted the resolutions and submitted them for approval, did not wish to subject the Hungarians, who suddenly became a minority, nor the Saxons, to the indignities they themselves were exposed to in the past. They declare "complete national freedom for the nationalities living together." This sounded very good, and continued: "Every nationality has the right to its own education and governance, in its own language, and its own administration by individuals elected from among themselves." This was clearly a declaration not only of individual, but collective nationality rights. It had been.

It was remarkable that the Transylvanian Romanian left wing did not support the union, or only gave lukewarm support to it. The reason for this was that at the time when the union was proclaimed, there was a much more liberal and increasingly left wing regime in Budapest to which 30 Social Democrats had been elected. Subsequently, the Entente moved substantial military forces into northern Hungary which made the pressures exerted by the victorious forces irresistible. The Entente was no longer concerned only with punishing the Hungarians for their participation in the war, but it satisfied increasing Romanian demands and promoted the prompt establishment of Romanian administrations, which in numerous locations and on numerous occasions used brute force. In exchange, the Entente expected to use Romanian armed forces in its projected military intervention in Soviet Russia. It is understandable that the Transylvanian Hungarians were becoming increasingly insecure, and that the Saxons and southern Svabians were beginning to think about protecting their own interests in the new Romanian era. They realized much sooner than the Hungarians that the game was over.

The Károlyi government couldn't carry the burden. The Entente and the Successor States separated from the Monarchy made increasingly impossible demands. The extreme left saw its chance and the Communists began to exert enormous pressure. The Károlyi government fell and the second, short-lived Soviet state, the Hungarian Soviet Republic, was established. (There will be a third one: in Bavaria...) If there were any illusions that the international Communists would be able to accomplish what the Social Democrats were unable to achieve before, during or after the war, in spite of their internationalism, these were rapidly dispelled. National awakening and separation became irresistible following the collapse of the Central European structure, severely weakened by four years of war. The Reds could make only pronouncements – possibly in good faith; they could create no new arrangements either between nations or between nationalities. Furthermore, when the Czechs intervened from the north and the Romanians from the east, the Hungarian Red Army, led mostly by officers of the former regime and composed of bled-out peasants and workers, went from defense to attack and fought very bravely to prevent the increasingly constricting lines of demarcation which left less and less of the Carpathian basin to the Hungarians, from becoming fixed borders. In vain; it was ordained otherwise.

In some of the Transylvanian cities the Soviet Republic, under Béla Kun, which originated in Kolozsvár, had some attraction, although it had little if any in the rural areas. The behavior of the Romanians was very much affected by the fact that the Hungarian Red Army included a Székely Division which openly wished to interfere in the determination of Transylvania's future. In fact, this division was rapidly broken up, and laid down its arms. In this it may have been a factor that the family members of the soldiers of this division were living in Székelyföld, under Romanian occupation, and as possible hostages.

The Kun regime that followed the Károlyi regime was also broken up and fled to Vienna. Royal Romania took advantage of the opportunities granted by the vacuum in power and its troops entered Budapest on August 4. They remained here until the middle of November, and then retired only to the Tisza, greedily expecting that this river would become the western border of Greater Romania. When on June 4, 1920 the peace treaty was signed in the Palace of Trianon outside Paris, almost one third of the former Hungary, 32% of its territory, slightly more than 100 thousand square kilometers, were given to Romania. (The mutilated Hungary retained only a total of 93 thousand square kilometers). Of the 5.25 million inhabitants of this region – some sources, erroneously gave this number as 3.5 million – 1.7 million were Hungarians and more than half a million were of German nationality. The great numerical superiority of the Romanians was evident. Yet, for instance, across from the city of Gyula and along the northern part of the common border, a significant area of purely Hungarian inhabitants came under Romanian control. At the same time – bilaterally – a number of cities were completely separated from their primary catchment areas. This resulted in enormous economic difficulties which have remained unresolved until this day.

Let us look at the demographic picture in somewhat greater detail according to the figures collected by András Rónai. The period in question, 1920, was not suitable for data collection, but valid conclusions can be drawn from the study of the 1910 and 1930 census results, both of which were obtained in peacetime. In the following, we present the data pertaining only to the territory ceded by the Trianon peace treaty.

1910:	Population	Percentage
Romanian	2,829,454	53.8
Hungarian	1,661,805	31.6
German	564,789	10.8
Serbo-Croatian	54,055	1.0
Czech-Slovakian	31,028	0.6
Russian-Ruthenian	20,482	0.4
Other	95,854	1.8
Total	5,257,467	100%

1930:	Population	Percentage
Romanian	3,237,000	58.3
Hungarian	1,483,000	26.7
German	543,000	9.8
Jewish	111,000	2.0
Gypsy	46,000	0.8
Other	130,000	2.4
Total	5,550,000	100%

Since Then

*E*ver since it became even a possibility that, in view of its Romanian majority, Transylvania may or should be removed from the aegis of the Hungarian Crown and be incorporated into a larger framework containing the bulk of the Romanian people – with its center naturally beyond the Carpathians – there had been no unanimity as to the mechanism of this change, even among the Romanians. The Romanians living inside the arc of the Carpathians would have preferred it if Transylvania were to enjoy a substantial autonomy. For this there are two strong indications. This part was economically, socially and politically more advanced than the potential incorporator. Secondly, under these conditions, the appreciable non Romanian residents would be more ready to accept a development that was clearly distressing for them. The residents of the Regát, however, wanted full integration, with a homogenous central administration, which did not recognize regional autonomies and in which the final say-so belonged to Bucharest, to the "old Romanian" politicians of the Regat.

In the gradual but rapid take-over of 1918-1919, initially there was some local autonomy and some evidence of toleration toward the nationalities. This was motivated by the practical realization that knowledge of the area and familiarity with the local conditions would facilitate the take-over. Thus, the Romanian representatives of the area were most suitable to manage its affairs. There was also a tactical consideration for such a move. The yet unsigned peace treaty would most likely be the more advantageous for the Romanian interests if the Entente decision makers were favorably impressed by the way the take-over was handled.

The moment the borders were determined in the Palace of Trianon, everything took on a different coloration. There was no further need for dissimulation. The liberal, democratizing trends and considerations were swept aside by the Regat majority. Complete incorporation began and remained in effect, even though there would always be ineradicable differences between Transylvania and Old Romania which would require a different approach and a different solution.

"Between the two world wars, Romania was a backward, agrarian country. This is well illustrated by the fact that in 1930, 78.7% of its active population worked in agriculture, and only 6.7% in industry. In agriculture dwarf-holdings and small farms predominated, and after the land reform, which was implemented in 1921, their preponderance increased. In industry and commerce, the large proportion of small enterprises was conspicuous. Oil extraction and coal mining together with iron and steel production characterized economic development in the longer run, as did, to some extent, the development of machine-tool industry. Besides Romanian capital, French, Belgian, German, and to a lesser degree, in Transylvania, Hungarian capital had a stake in the larger industrial enterprises, as well as in banks.

"As was typical in eastern Europe at this time, Romania's social structure bore the marks of economic underdevelopment. This meant that the peasantry constituted the majority of the population, and broad sections of it lived in traditonal, backward circumstances; standards of living were extraordinarily low. The working class, which was comparatively undeveloped, lived in a geographically limited area, and was concentrated in only a few branches of industry. Small businessmen, small traders and white collar workers made up the equivalent of the bourgeoisie. The state was directed by representatives of big business and by the large landowners." (Béla Köpeczi.)

The fairly extensive 1921 land reform – initiated after a war and among a population suffering from severe poverty in spite of the increase in the size of the country – was a historical necessity. This was a fact that was recognized by the Romanian leadership, while it was ignored by the Hungarian elite. Its results varied on a regional basis. In the Regat it improved the general structure of land ownership while in Transylvania it resulted in a shift between the land owned by a majority group and the land held by the members of the minority nationalities. There is no question as to who benefited. It did not exclude, however, all Hungarians and other nationalities from acquiring land. The loss of the jointly owned forests and pastures was a particularly severe blow, since they played a major role in the economic life of the Székely communities.

In the strongly conservative Romanian leadership, the promoters of an autarchic economic evolution set the tone. This path was partially justified by the fact that the new Romania was almost completely surrounded by countries – Soviet Russia, Bulgaria and Hungary – who all lost territory to it. At that time only the narrow Czechoslovak-Romanian border was a "friendly" one. Against autarchy, there was the possibility of an internationally protected maritime and Danubian shipping industry. Its expenses were largely covered by the increasing production of oil in the eastern foothills of the Carpathians, which made Romania the world's fifth largest producer in the early 1930s. (The autarchic trend was continued in the Romanian "socialist" economic developments after 1945, just as the industrial-armament program of Kálmán Darányi in Hungary, the so-called Győr Program was fully realized only much later, during the feverish Rákosi-Gerő industrialization.)

Romanian industrial developments at this time – contrary to the events after 1945 – took place almost exclusively in the Regat, in spite of the fact that the available manpower in this area was much less skilled when compared to the Transylvanian one. The new Romanian industry had an effect on the demography of the country and led to migrations. Between 1918 and 1923 about 200 thousand Transylvanian Hungarians fled to the mother country – mostly officials and intellectuals – the new migration toward the east was triggered by the demand for workers in the industries of Old Romania. As a consequence of this two-way migration, thousands of the escapees to Hungary lived in great poverty, in old railroad cars on the sidings of railway freight depots, while Bucharest became a city with one of the world's largest Hungarian populations. Many Transylvanian Hungarians, while preserving their original homes, commuted to temporary or permanent jobs in Old Romania, mostly in construction work and in industry. The emigration to America, interrupted by the war, was also resumed.

The economy of certain regions, small areas or cities, sensitively documented the absurdity of the new borders. While in the south and in the north the incorporation of Hungarian national blocks may be explained, to some extent, by geographic and economic (rivers and railroads) circumstances, the new western Hungarian-Romanian border was most idiosyncratic and most economically damaging. Nagyvárad, for example, which was only a few kilometers from the new border and its population – at that time still predominantly Hungarian – was devastated by the loss of its natural economic and commercial base in the Great Plains. If Trianon had not paralyzed the growth of this city, it would have rapidly become the second largest Hungarian city after Budapest. Its development after 1945 was purely artificial, and even today it can barely subsist on the resources of its former area. This was and is to the great detriment of both Hungarian and Romanian economy.

Even though the loss in manpower after 1918 was substantial, this was not the real tragedy of the Transylvanian Hungarians. It was the fate of those who remained behind. The changes were dramatic. The Transylvania Hungarian society and its every class, level and group had become a minority in the area that for a thousand years it called home. It had to learn the miseries of this fact. The lovely promises of Gyulafehérvár disappeared. It was of no great benefit that a large part of its elite remained obstinately faithful and did not take advantage of the available and, for it, very promising opportunities of emigration. The literary life was rich and manifold. Periodical publications [*Pásztortűz* (Campfire), *Erdélyi Helikon* (Transylvanian Helicon), and the left-wing *Korunk* (Our Times)] organized around the Erdélyi Szépmíves Céh (Transylvanian Craftsmen's Guild), which was able to distribute the best works of the Transylvanian authors, in Hungary, in sizable editions. There was also a slowly developing, gently naive Transylvanian spirit, concerning the exemplary spiritual role of the Transylvanian Hungarians.

The ongoing Romanization which they later used, contrary to all evidence, as justification for the declaration of a national state took many forms. It granted economic advantages and increased employment for officials from the Regat, who poured in to fill the vacancies left by the withdrawal of the Hungarians but, most significantly, the major emphasis was placed on the use of the Romanian language, both in official and personal communications and on the complete restructuring and rearranging of the schools and of the educational process.

Considering the latter, it seems appropriate to recognize the diligence and the rate with which, in the framework of the revitalized educational system, the Romanians developed their own, new officials and intellectuals. The strengthening of public education obviously also served to replace the teaching of the Hungarian language, or to relegate it to religious instruction. This, incidentally, also had the effect of tying the Transylvanian nationalities much more tightly to their Church and to its institutions – contrary to the secularization of the last one-hundred years. This action-reaction was further emphasized by the strong support that the two great national Romanian Churches, but particularly the Greek Orthodox, acting almost as a recognized state religion, gave to the national and nationalistic endeavors of their country.

During the 1920s and 1930s the "mutilated" Hungary blamed Trianon for all economic and social problems and troubles. These included the loss of territory, of forests and of most sources of raw materials. These were indeed grievous losses. Yet in the so spectacularly enlarged Romania, the economic concerns and the social tensions were no less. There were a series of peasant movements – sometimes bloody – in both Transylvania and Old Romania, and there were labor unrests and resistance against greedy domestic and foreign robber capitalism. It is understandable that among the doubly disenfranchised – economically and as minorities – there was a strong, radical left wing. In the Transylvanian and in the entire Romanian Communist movement there were numerous Hungarians and Jews who considered themselves Hungarians. This had serious effects after 1945.

The rebellious social dissatisfaction assuredly did not limit itself to a move to the left. It also gave munition to the right wing, which came naturally to the ruling classes, traditionally influenced by a nationalist public sentiment. The main battle in the Romanian political arena was between the various factions of the right wing. Some of them were Populists, others relied heavily on the elite.

It is not surprising that the world-wide economic depression hit Romania's undeveloped economy particularly hard. This also showed the limitations imposed by autarchy. The great recession came at a time when the Iron Guard, supported by the Orthodox clergy and many of the university students, was already ready and waiting. This movement started in Moldavia and would very soon have a major effect on all of Romania. This bloody movement, responsible for political murders and for anti-Semitic pogroms (it tried to recruit even in Transylvania with vague promises of autonomy), showed peculiar similarities with and differences from its European counterparts. Both its overt and covert activities were more extensive than those of the Hungarian extreme right, the Arrow Cross. While the latter got a tragic and criminal starring role "only" in the last act of the Hungarian tragedy in 1944-45, the Iron Guards were attacked first in 1930 and then again in 1941 and – similarly to the elimination of the SA leadership in Germany in 1934 – there were two "Nights of the Long Knives" in which other right wing Romanian groups brutally and bloodily tried to do away with them.

In these turbulent extremes of Romanian public life, the political freedom of movement for the Hungarians in Transylvania was very limited. Even with the tightly controlled educational system, they could still serve the preservation of their nationality. Hungarian culture and science were supported by institutions that came and went but were maintained more effectively by the most talented writers, artists and scientists who gained substantial recognition both in Transylvania and in Hungary. The attempts to form political parties on a nationality basis were generally feeble and in 1938, all parties in Romania were disbanded and the multi-party system was replaced by a corporate form of statism.

The situation of the German nationalities in Transylvania, the Saxons and, further south in the Banate, the Svabians was somewhat more favorable. Ever since Gyulafehérvár they resigned themselves to the Romanian conquest. Their *Lebensraum,* or "living space", was far removed from that of their Great German homeland, and could hardly be expected to form a union with it. Also, Romania exchanged its former French-English orientation with a German one. This naturally agreed with Hitler's desires to exert a tighter control over Romanian oil.

The Transylvanian Germans, who were generally receptive to the Hitlerian ideas, became the favorites of the Romanian leadership, since the Romanians viewed their relationship with this group as the touchstone of their future relationship with the Third Reich. Yet, the above could hardly explain the dramatic twists and turns that took place in this region in 1940. The outbreak of World War II put a land mine under everything that seemed settled "in perpetuity" by the Parisian peace treaties. A number of European borders were moved. Hungary, which received a significant area from Slovakia under the First Vienna Agreement in the fall of 1938 and which, after Czechoslovakia's destruction by Hitler, occupied the Kárpátalja – and re-established a common border with Poland – thereafter increasingly looked toward Transylvania. The Horthy regime, whose primary purpose, since the moment of its inception, was the territorial revision of the Trianon treaty, would not have been true to itself if it did not prepare for this – with military forces, if necessary.

Hitler, however, needed Hungarian wheat, meat, aluminum and the Transdanubian oil just as much as he needed the Ploesti oil. Pál Teleki, serving his second term as Prime Minister, was concerned about Hungary gaining back the territories taken away by Trianon, purely by the grace of Germany. The Hungarian-Romanian revisionary conference, held in Turnu-Severin in the summer of 1940, and instigated solely by Germany, ended in complete failure. It was the Second Vienna Agreement, engineered by a German-Italian "tribunal" that gave northern Transylvania, i.e., the northern and eastern parts of Greater Transylvania, back to Hungary. At the same time, Romania was made to give up about 50 thousand square kilometers in the north to the Soviet Union. In the south, it had to yield 7,000 square kilometers to Bulgaria and the area it had to cede to Hungary encompassed another 44 thousand square kilometers. This was truly a Romanian Trianon. It was that, even though, this time it was a new country and not a thousand-year-old kingdom that was being dismembered by its neighbors, under the authority granted by foreign great powers. The ruling king, Charles II, was deposed, and was replaced by his son, Michael I.

There are as many estimates about the population and its ethnic composition of the area returned to Hungary as there are sources for same. Reasonably accurate estimates can be made only prospectively from the 1930 Romanian census and, retrospectively from the 1941 Hungarian one. We can be certain, however, that of a population on one million, the Romanians amounted to more than 40%, while in the part retained by Romania, they represented only 60%, which also included the German nationalities, the majority of whom live in that area.

The new borders, drawn up by the Second Vienna Agreement, were not satisfactory to either party, and were replete with economic and transportational absurdities. Thus, the almost totally Hungarian Székelyföld could not be reached from Hungary by rail. One of the explanations of these absurdities was that the division of the territory, largely determined by the Germans – Ciano, the Italian Foreign Minister was only a bit-player in the negotiations – had a hidden agenda item. Based primarily on the Transylvanian Saxons and on the Serbs in the Banate, the Germans wanted to control an economic belt in this area which was significant in itself and also represented a bridge toward the Ploesti oil fields and Bucharest. In this, the Germans also relied on the chain of southern Transdanubian and eastern Great Plains German villages.

Romania could not resist the Vienna decisions. During the previous weeks the Hungarian army, although poorly equipped, was ready to fight. It now clumsily completed the task of occupying the region, welcomed enthusiastically by the Hungarian population. It encountered no resistance. The stories about confrontations and bloodletting in Transylvania, published much later, but cited frequently even today, are rumors and fabrications.

The enthusiasm cooled off rapidly. Tensions developed between the Hungarians who remained in place and held out during the Romanian occupation, and who now expected to play a leading role, and the military leaders and administrators dispatched to Transylvania from Hungary. Prime Minister Pál Teleki had very little success with his confidential instructions in which he advised moderation in the treatment of the Romanians who suddenly again became a minority nationality from previously having been a nation. The new Hungarian regime in Transylvania, or rather northern Transylvania, was most effective in using its local people in destroying the Communist organizations. The less prominent leftists who managed to escape imprisonment quickly found themselves serving in labor battalions, under military direction, together with several thousand Romanians. Large population migrations took place among both Hungarians and Romanians, between northern and southern Transylvania. The Hungarian wartime boom and the resulting serious demands for workers resulted in that many were put to work in the Csepel factories, first as volunteers and later, another group, under compulsion. At the same time the situation of the approximately half million Hungarians in southern Transylvania took a marked turn for the worse. (This number represented about 15% of the local population, with another 15% being Germans).

One certainly could and should write the history of the next four years in Transylvania. The further course of World War II, however, and the divergent politics of Hungary and Romania have made this, at best, an episode without any foreseeable influence on the future. While both the claimants for Transylvania, Hungary and Romania entered the war on Hitler's – and each other's – side, they did this largely to obtain and keep Transylvania. Through overt and covert channels, both countries received word from the increasingly victorious Allied Powers that at the end of the war, Transylvania would be awarded to the one who would wrest it away from Germany. This was confirmed by the Soviet Union via the Hungarian Communist emigrés in Moscow, because of – or in spite of – the fact that the Soviet Union itself had territorial demands against Romania. This had now become the position of the Western Powers as well who conceded that they could not avoid or prevent Eastern Central Europe from falling under Soviet influence.

When at the end of August, 1944 Romania which had fought on Hitler's side with considerable forces, first asked for an armistice and then, two days later, declared war on Germany, the fate of Transylvania was once again decided. There was no turning back. The Romanian army was successfully turned around and the country moved from the rank of the losers to the camp of the winners. Their only gain was northern Transylvania. She did not regain the other

territories lost in 1941, and this is a grievance to
Romania to this day.

The Hungarian army, having suffered very heavy
losses between the millstones of the Soviet front,
had tried, as best it could, to strengthen the crest line
of the Carpathians which in the north and east constituted the borders of Hungary. The terrain lent
itself very well to this purpose. Yet, the rapidly moving Soviet troops, including their new allies, used
the passes of the Southern Carpathians to enter
Transylvania. The Hungarian army was unsuccessful
in preventing this, in spite of counter-attacks, first
from the Kolozsvár area and then, with German
assistance, from the southern Great Plains, in the
direction Arad-Temesvár. Every attempt collapsed in
days or weeks. The fight shifted very shortly to the
central portion of the Hungarian Great Plains, where
in the region of Debrecen – already to the west of
Transylvania – the Debrecen Tank Battle was fought.
This is an almost forgotten incident of World War II,
although considering the forces involved, it was a
very major engagement.

Thus, when after much hesitation, Miklós Horthy's
clumsy and weak armistice effort was made on
October 15, 1944 and the Hungarian Arrow Cross
(Fascists) assumed power, most of northern Transylvania was already in Soviet and Romanian hands.
The war rolled on bloodily toward the west. Behind
it, first in the Székelyföld and then in all of northern
Transylvania, the Romanian administration was
being organized. This did not prevent the atrocities,
the cruel, bloody, anti-Hungarian pogroms in several
settlements of the Székelyföld and in the area of

Kolozsvár. Such events were common behind the fronts during periods of transition. The culprits were the Maniu Guardists who were the successors of the Iron Guard. Iuliu Maniu (1873-?1951) was twice Prime Minister, the leader of the National Peasant Party, one of the leaders of the liberal wing of the Romanian right. He was not responsible for the murder and persecution of the Hungarians perpetrated under his name, but he did not distance himself from them either. The situation deteriorated to the point where the Soviet military command, not exactly celebrated for its sensitivity, took over the administration of northern Transylvania for four months – nominally under the auspices of the four power Allied Control Commission. "These four transitional months represented a strange historic moment; the life of northern Transylvania, its reconstruction and its political life, were organized and directed by Romanian and Hungarian Communists. The latter had their power base in the local and county organizations of the Hungarian Popular Association. In both Hungary and Romania, the Communists at this time were just beginning the struggle to strengthen their position." (Béla Köpeczi.)

There were a few Hungarians, who had hopes during these four months that not everything had been decided yet. It was. There are Romanians who believe that this early Communist "take-over" – triggered by the activities of the Maniu Guardists – was instituted by the Hungarian Communists who were later considered as the managers of the subsequent Soviet orientation. A Romanian administration was set up again, and Petru Groza (1884-1958) formed a government in Bucharest. He did this among quasi civil war conditions in Romanian politics and with the support of the Soviet Union which, in Romania, was even more manipulative than in the other countries occupied by it. Groza's principal promises were rapid land reform and Romanian control over the administration of northern Transylvania.

Groza remains a controversial figure. He completed some of his studies in Budapest, spoke Hungarian well and was very fond of the almost legendary Hungarian poet of the turn of the century, Endre Ady. He promised in very liberal speeches that the Romanian-Hungarian relationships would be placed on a new basis. In spite of these nice – and, perhaps, honestly meant – words, under his rule as Prime Minister the mass internments, confiscations, and deprivations of civil rights of the Hungarians continued "without interference". The "legal framework" for these actions was the concept that virtually the entire German minority and a large number of Hungarian adult males were considered to be war criminals and enemies of the Romanian people and of the Romanian state.

Confronted with these harsh realities, Groza's proposals for regional federations, customs unions and the "spiritualization" of the borders, were worth very little. It is even possible that the appealing declarations and proposals had no real intent behind them and were made only to serve as a base for the peace treaties and to assure favorable recognition of Romania by the West.

At the end of December 1947, we had the odd situation where a country, which came under Soviet

influence at the end of World War II, was still a kingdom. Petru Groza and the Communist Gheorghiu-
Dej (1901-1965), a local product and not a Moscow
emigré, put an end to this, forcing King Michael to
abdicate and to leave the country. The Romanian
People's Republic was proclaimed. This then formally prepared the ground for Romania to become integrated into the increasingly homogenized group of
Soviet satellites. At this time, it was the integration
that was impressive. Later, a relative separation
becomes prominent. Even later, this was viewed as a
meritorious event.

At the same time, Hungary, as a consequence of
the internal power struggle of the Communists,
increasingly leaned toward the Moscow emigré
group, the first leader of the Romanian Communists,
Gheorghiu-Dej, gained his position primarily at the
expense of the former Muscovite comrades and
non-Romanian rivals. About the middle of 1952 he
added the post of Prime Minister to that of First
Secretary, while Groza was "kicked upstairs" and
was given the presidency of the Parliament – a largely ceremonial position.

When we consider those massive, but largely mis-
directed economic, cultural and political changes
which convulsed, with minor variations, all the
"Socialist" countries, they really facilitated the segre-
gational and/or integrational nationality policies
which persist with some ups and downs in Romania
to this day. Even under the extreme rule of
Gheorghiu-Dej, there were indications that some of
the issues could be normalized. Namely, there were
provisions in the new constitution, which was mod-

eled after the Soviet one, but which contained certain nationality rights. Accordingly, the area of the former regions of Csík, Erdőszentgyörgy, Gyergyószentmiklós, Kézdivásárhely, Maroshévíz, Marosvásárhely, Régen, Sepsiszentgyörgy and Székelyudvarhely were united into the Hungarian Autonomous Province. "The Hungarian Autonomous Province (MAT) encompassed the largest area inhabited by Hungarians, it represented only about one third of the entire Hungarian population of Romania. According to the 1956 census the MAT had a total population of 731,387 of which 77.3% (565,510) were Hungarians and 20.1% (146,830) were Romanians. The proclaimed autonomy became totally illusory, since the Provincial Statutes under which the laws were to be administered, were never enacted." (Andrea R. Süle.)

MAT was finally disbanded in 1968, just at the time when otherwise, transiently perhaps, some nationality rights and opportunities beckoned. Let us keep, however, to the time sequence. The forced industrialization was no longer limited to the Regat and reached Transylvania, resulting in the influx of large numbers of Romanian workers. In the meantime, the still better educated and more skillful Hungarian – and German – workers could not be spared. For the higher positions, however, the non-Romanians had a much better chance if they moved beyond the Carpathians and away from the land of their co-nationals.

After all the escapes to Hungary after 1945, Transylvania's manpower loss was further aggravated by a significant move to the Regat. Another, demographically even more natural phenomenon, was the increase of mixed marriages. In these cases it was usually the Hungarian spouse who wanted the children to be raised as Romanians to spare them the miseries of belonging to a minority nationality. In the "socialist" countries everything was done according to "The Plan". It can be considered to be according to a plan, (without quotation marks), that in Transylvania the Romanians were favored not only in industry, but also in educational, hospital and office positions, while the new minority intellectuals were enticed to move to Romanian areas with offers of employment or were forcibly moved to such areas. It was frequently easier to be a Hungarian in Bucharest than in Kolozsvár or in Nagyvárad.

It was the practice in Hungary at this time that the enlisted army personnel was stationed as far away from their homes as possible. In Romania, this same practice resulted in Hungarian boys serving in the Regat, or in the Danube delta – a huge concentration camp – while the Transylvanian barracks were filled to the rafters with Romanian enlisted personnel.

In public education, the principal issue was the preservation of the national language in instruction in the face of determined efforts to curtail this. Highlighting higher education, the Transylvanian Hungarian population, by virtue of its numbers, would be entitled to several universities, and a number of disciplines and professions could be taught rationally. Yet in 1959 the only Hungarian University, in Kolozsvár, established in 1872 and named after the Bolyais, was coerced into a merger which terminated its separate existence. They also gradually limited, or did not appropriately expand Hungarian professional education, and thus forced the Hungarians, trying to better themselves, into the industrial arena, already over-developed according to Romanian and "socialist" principles.

In spite of all this, there was a considerable increase in Hungarian books and other publications, both in Transylvania and in all of Romania. As far as content was concerned, however, this was subjected to and crippled by such a rigid censorship as we had never experienced in Hungary. It was part of the whole picture that the intelligencia – primarily the authors – whom they allowed to speak, were kept amenable by relatively generous honoraria. The Transylvanian Hungarian writers, those who published, lived at a much higher economic standard than their counterparts in Hungary. What was more important, however, was the tragedy of the silenced, maladjusted and emotionally crippled creative artists. The emigration which continues to this day is a greater loss to Transylvania – in the natural course of events – than it is a gain to the host country, even though the latter is not insignificant.

After Stalin's death in 1953, the imposition of uniformity on the Communist camp stopped, and then was cautiously reversed. In the case of Romania, this was manifested in the establishment of an individual path which – surprisingly – led to the Romanization of the country's foreign policy, a matter usually tightly controlled by the Soviet leadership. The internal policies remained insensitive toward internal demands.

It was also astonishing to what degree the Soviet Union tolerated Romania following its own path. For us it is of particular significance that while in 1956 the armored units sent to crush the Hungarian revolt came to Budapest from Temesvár, in 1958, Romania "took in" the deported Imre Nagy and his associates after the Yugoslav betrayal. In 1958 the Soviet troops were withdrawn from Romania. This suggests that the Soviet leadership was hardly concerned about a Romanian turnaround after this gesture. It also suggests that the Romanian leadership had self-confidence, and believed that it could maintain its rule without the assistance of Soviet bayonets. It proved this for three additional decades, but at the cost of an ever increasing and increasingly repressive dictatorship.

We now come to the penultimate chapter of our history. After Gheorghiu-Dej's death in March 1965, power was assumed by the 47-year-old Nicolae Ceausescu, who in the Soviet type gerontocratic hierarchy was considered a youngster. Even though he acted like a modest and loyal spear-carrier during the life of his former chief, he soon found a way of making his predecessor and his group responsible for all the ills of the country. The merry-go-round of personnel changes that characterized his entire rule began at this time, and became increasingly idiosyncratic. In the beginning he was forced to try to find some common ground with the nationalities and the first few years of his rule brought a certain moderation. Later on, he became the typical expression of traditional Romanian nationalism. He inscribed himself among the "great builders" of history. In this he caused more harm than just the irrational use of the natural resources or the crippling effects of forced labor on hundreds of thousands of human beings. In his radical building program in Bucharest, whole historically and artistically important quarters were leveled and even the historic buildings of the still favored Orthodox Church were demolished. The same megalomanic building and societal restructuring drive targeted hundreds of small settlements in Transylvania for destruction. It did, or should have, become necessary for the population to move to the futuristic urban developments.

It was at this time that a paradoxical advantage was fatally threatened. With the exception of the Székelyföld, the least agriculturally productive parts of Transylvania were spared the imposition of collective farming organizations. In spite of the inclement climate, the poor soil and the manifold administrative restrictions, the private agricultural enterprise, left to its own devices in these areas, produced relative prosperity. Fortunately, the destruction of villages began only at the very end of the maniacal dictator's life. Its tragic potential was demonstrated, but was not carried to completion.

Among the demographic and migratory processes affecting Romania and, quite particularly Transylvania, there was one chapter in Ceausescu's "nationality policy" that was highly "successful". Namely, the way he permitted the Romanian Jews and the German nationals to emigrate in return for a substantial head tax. This was a true "ethnic cleansing" which also showed a very large financial profit. While it is obviously a highly questionable affair, perhaps it is a rational decision on the part of Israel and Germany to pay the price which, disguised as compensation for the cost of education and care, was in fact a ransom for the people who had become hostages. The number of people thus redeemed was very large. Since many of the Jews and most of the Germans (Saxons and Svabians) who were allowed to leave the country came from Transylvania, this had a marked effect on the ethnic composition of the region. The multinationality was decreased and the Romanian-Hungarian duality was strengthened. The third ethnic group, which just recently began to consider themselves a separate nationality, the Gypsies, complicated the situation, particularly since their numbers were growing rapidly. The Romanian Gypsy problem was even more serious and difficult in the Regat.

Beyond the Lajta, for a long time, they did not know or did not wish to notice that the Romanian affairs were becoming increasingly bizarre and would be worthwhile subjects for a Kafka or an Orwell. When during the 1970s, as part of the Romanian cultural revolution, the Ceausescu regime issued ordinances for the better protection of the national treasures, they did not realize that this would entail the "nationalization" of irreplaceable museum and archival treasures which under rigid centralized control would be lost forever to scientific inquiry particularly if they did not seem to be supportive of the various historic, demographic and other theories which were raised to the level of Romanian political creed.

When they forbade that a citizen of a foreign country stay overnight in a private home – this projected a ban of a foreigner even entering such a home – and further demanded a detailed accounting of any contact with a foreign national, this made it impossible for the minorities to have direct contact with family members from abroad. It was a clear violation of human rights and was even made worse by classifying such contacts as a seditious act and treason. In practice these dreadful ordinances were never rigidly enforced, but their existence in this century in Europe is almost unimaginable. Similar tendencies were shown only in Albania.

Yet, Romania was consistently thought of by the West as the Cinderella of the Eastern block. The reason for this can be found in the fact that Romania resisted Soviet demands in some areas and did not always conform to the pattern of Satellite behavior. It did not break diplomatic relations with China and with Israel, and its athletes participated in the Los Angeles Olympic games. Even more importantly, in 1968 it vigorously opposed the Warsaw Pact Nations' intervention against Prague. It did this under the principle of national sovereignty and non interference into the internal affairs of another country. In fact, it did these things to be able to preserve its own internal dictatorship, free from foreign threats and interference. This, according to the ideas and illusions of the Ceausescu clan, prevented the Czechoslovakian type of détente which was a major nightmare in Romania. They were wrong. But not entirely.

Ceausescu's megalomania kept the country from falling into debt, because every burden was piled onto the back of the peoples of Romania. Europe of the 1980s cannot even imagine the deprivations – food rationing, intermittent power outages, the limitations of heating fuel, causing freezing home temperatures – that they had to suffer for years on end. The cup of suffering overflowed in 1989, although the background and the details of the events taking place at the end of that year are still shrouded in mystery. It seems likely that one part of the Romanian leadership was getting ready for just such an event. This group noting the cracks in the Eastern block, and being concerned about the increasingly important Western attitudes, began to view the activities and absurdities of the dynastic Ceausescu clan and its Praetorian Guard as a major burden. Their preparations for a power take-over were disturbed, but their activities were accelerated by the popular movement developing on behalf of László Tőkés, the Hungarian Reformed Minister of Temesvár, who was sentenced to dismissal from his congregation for criticizing the system. The brutal police-military activities directed against this movement turned out to have been exaggerated by the reports generated during the rapidly evolving events. There is no doubt, however, that at Christmas in Temesvár the seeds of a popular rebellion were germinating. Such a popular uprising was fully justified by the crimes committed against the Hungarian minority and against the people of Romania in general. The counter-attack of the regime, which was already under way, threatened the outbreak of a civil war. Yet, events took a different turn.

For reasons not entirely clear, within days and even hours, the center of gravity of the events was transferred from Temesvár to Bucharest, which for this and other reasons also developed a revolutionary atmosphere. The events, under way, took a different direction and there was also a shift in emphasis. This was further influenced by the fact that Ceausescu, flying back from abroad, completely misunderstood the situation and acted accordingly. Everything came together and resulted in an almost bloodless, very peculiar coup d'état – coup d'état whose only bloody and brutal act was the summary court-martial of the Ceausescu couple and their immediate execution, shown on television. This had a shocking effect that may well have been responsible for preventing a civil war.

The December 1989 coup d'état resulted in effect in an obvious change of the system, even though this was almost certainly not the original intent but was mandated by the pressures of the day. Was it the intent? Perhaps? Yet, that it turned out in this way was due primarily to events that took place outside Romania and to geopolitical and world political factors that influenced the instigators of the coup d'état.

The evolving multi-party system and the new parliamentary framework made it possible for parties to develop along the lines of nationalities and ethnicity. This increased freedom to the point where justified ethnic endeavors got mixed up with party politics. At the same time the activities of the parties serving minority ethnic interests are impeded by the phalanx of Romanian parties who may differ from each other in some areas but who are as one in their nationalistic sentiments.

It must be emphasized that the terror of the Ceausescu era, its intellectual-ideological, political and economic absurdities were not limited to the Hungarians and to other minorities. This regime, extreme even in the Eastern block, was a Romanian national tragedy. Since the various changes have taken place, the minority concerns have come out into the open but have not been resolved. Even where the conditions have improved there is the continuous threat of the fundamentalist Greater Romania ideals. Under this heading, there is a real possibility of further restrictions of the minorities.

During the mid 1980s, and particularly since 1989, further tens of thousands have left, are leaving, or escaping from Transylvania. They are going to Hungary or further to the West to emigrate or, at least, for temporary work. Their reception in the mother country is ambiguous. The population of Hungary has been decreasing due to high mortality combined with a low birth rate. Thus, the "blood transfusion" created by the immigrants should be welcome. Transylvanian immigrants and migrant workers also take jobs that are left vacant by the native Hungarians. This trend, incidentally, is not new. With some interruptions, it has been going on since the 1920s. The migration, if viewed from the perspective of Transylvania, is alarming since it further erodes the number of Hungarians in Transylvania. There are also considerable numbers of Romanians who are pleased to work, or would like to work and settle in Hungary. This suggests that the migration is largely an economic matter and only secondarily due to nationality issues.

In conclusion, we must add something to this history of Transylvania which had been approached intentionally from a Hungarian point of view. Namely, that the history of Romania for the past 100-150 years is undoubtedly a success story. For us, its most significant component is that it moved Transylvania beyond the territory of Hungary. It is a fascinating example of the creation of a national state, in the most recent times, taking full advantage of opportunities and not necessarily ensuing from historical circumstances or precedents. A thousand years from now Romania may recall these times in the same way that we think back to the conquest by Árpád and the founding of the country by St. Stephen. It is a bitter and insoluble problem for the Hungarians that this successful creation of a country had to take place in opposition to us and largely at our expense. It remains only a hope today what the poet Attila József, who was partly of Romanian extraction, wrote in 1936: "The battles fought by our ancestors / are transmuted into peace by remembrance..."

And last but not least, while the limitations in space prevent me from including the extensive bibliography of my source materials, I must emphasize the outstanding assistance I have received from *The History of Transylvania*, edited by Béla Köpeczi and published in Hungarian by the Akadémia Kiadó in Budapest.

Index